The Politics of Not Speaking

The Politics of Not Speaking

ELAD LAPIDOT

Cover Credit: Steve Sabelia, "Till The End." Black & White Photo Emulsion on Jerusalem Stone. 19 × 15.5 × 6.5 cm. 2004. UNIQUE. An artwork from the series is in the British Museum Collection in London.

Published by State University of New York Press, Albany

© 2025 State University of New York

All rights reserved

Printed in the United States of America

No part of this book may be used or reproduced in any manner whatsoever without written permission. No part of this book may be stored in a retrieval system or transmitted in any form or by any means including electronic, electrostatic, magnetic tape, mechanical, photocopying, recording, or otherwise without the prior permission in writing of the publisher.

Links to third-party websites are provided as a convenience and for informational purposes only. They do not constitute an endorsement or an approval of any of the products, services, or opinions of the organization, companies, or individuals. SUNY Press bears no responsibility for the accuracy, legality, or content of a URL, the external website, or for that of subsequent websites.

For information, contact State University of New York Press, Albany, NY
www.sunypress.edu

Library of Congress Cataloging-in-Publication Data

Name: Lapidot, Elad, author.
Title: The politics of not speaking / Elad Lapidot.
Description: Albany : State University of New York Press, [2025] | Includes
    bibliographical references and index.
Identifiers: LCCN 2024025732 | ISBN 9798855801149 (hardcover : alk. paper) |
    ISBN 9798855801156 (ebook) | ISBN 9798855801132 (pbk. : alk. paper)
Subjects: LCSH: Speech—Philosophy. | Communication in politics.
Classification: LCC P95 .L37 2025 | DDC 302.2/242—dc23/eng/20240806
LC record available at https://lccn.loc.gov/2024025732

Contents

Acknowledgments	vii
Introduction	1
Chapter 1. Politics as Break of Logos: Carl Schmitt	5
Chapter 2. Dialogue as Violence: Martin Heidegger	17
Chapter 3. Decolonialism as Logoclasm: Frantz Fanon	35
Corollary I: On BDS: On the Boycott, Divestment, Sanctions (BDS) Movement	53
Chapter 4. Can't Speak: Gayatri Chakravorty Spivak	59
Chapter 5. No One Language: Jacques Derrida	77
Corollary II: On Jewish-Christian Dialogue	97
Not Last Words	101
Notes	113
References	115
Index	117

Acknowledgments

The following chapters are transcripts of five talks that were delivered on July 25–29, 2022, in the Parrhesia School of Philosophy at the *Vierte Welt, Kottbusser Tor*, Berlin. The texts have been slightly edited, but without changing their quality of spontaneous oral speech. The volume also contains two corollaries, namely two discussions of specific contemporary themes that arise from the more general conceptual analyses, as well as a concluding section, which are based on three written lectures that were delivered, respectively, at the University of Basel and at the University of Haifa in the spring and fall of 2022, and at the EHESS Paris in the spring of 2024.

I am grateful to the participants of these talks for their invaluable comments and questions, some of which I have incorporated into the text. Special thanks go to Steve Corcoran, the director of the Parrhesia School of Philosophy and a dear friend, for organizing these talks. I would also like to thank Rachel Pafe, who patiently transcribed the talks, and Veronica O'Neill, who meticulously and sensitively edited the text. I would like to express my gratitude to the *Centre d'Études en Civilisations, Langues et Lettres Étrangères* (Cecille) and to the University of Lille for their generous support of this publication.

Introduction

Over the next five days and sessions, I will guide you through some important texts and thinkers. Through five different texts, we circle around the theme of "the politics of not speaking." Today I will start by saying a little about this question and open up other ideas that will be developed over the course of our time together.

On a conceptual level, when we think about politics it is often understood as deeply connected to language: speaking, communicating, talking, discussing, reasoning, arguing, debating, and so on. Sometimes when I talk about such terms I use a word that you may have already heard, *logos*. Logos has different meanings in different contexts. It originally comes from the Greek verb *logein*, which means "speaking." While logos does mean something like speech or speaking, over the centuries it has become synonymous with reasoning and in some respects also related to knowing or science. I use logos in the context of speaking or talking as an expression of trying to find, for example, reasonable solutions. This means speaking in the sense of what humans do and what expresses their being as reasonable, knowledgeable, thinking creatures. Everything we talk about here is somehow connected to the relationship between politics and logos, which I sometimes call "logo-politics." This term denotes the relationship between politics—how we think about politics, how we enact politics, how we construct or criticize politics—and how we do language. It denotes how we understand language, how we speak, how we perform language, and language more specifically as communication, as a way of understanding, a means of being reasonable in a community. Thus, everything we are talking about is connected to logo-politics.

I start by presenting two models, or paradigms, for how we potentially can and usually do understand the relationship between politics and

2 | Politics of Not Speaking

language: two models of logo-politics. The first, which is perhaps more common today, is the understanding of politics as based on speaking, on logos. Politics is thus about connecting people in a rational way and creating a space of discussion, conversation, and dialogue. Politics is about speaking via arguing, conversing, reasoning, discussing, debating, and so forth. Throughout history there is at least one very important reference for this idea, Aristotle. Aristotle is one of the first philosophers to ever speak about politics, arguably the philosopher who coined the word "politics" as we understand it in philosophy today. From the very beginning of his *Politics*, to explain what politics is and what it means for humans doing politics, Aristotle connects it to the capacity of human beings to reason, or, as he calls it, to do logos, *logein*, to speak in a reasoned way. Aristotle builds the whole idea of politics on logos, a certain paradigm that is still prevalent today.

When today we think about our societies, our systems, and often call them democratic, we are speaking very centrally about institutions or spaces of speaking. For example, parliament, which is understood as the central institution of democracy, is basically an institution of *parler*, an institution of talking. The public sphere has been understood as an important institution, an important space of democracy, of politics, and of everything that allows this sphere of discussion to exist. We speak about freedom of speech and freedom of the press, and we understand the flow of speaking, reasoning, and talking as something basic for our political systems. There are a number of examples of how we understand our political systems to be based on free speech and speaking, dialogue and understanding. These ideas fall under the first model of speaking: politics as speaking.

The second model I want to present is almost the opposite, whereby politics is about not speaking. This is in fact the title of the seminar, which is focused precisely on reflecting about how politics is about not speaking. We will see that there are different ways of understanding not speaking besides a complete absence of speech, complete silence. Even though Aristotle's model or paradigm of politics is built on the aforementioned idea of logos, even if our coordinated collective existence is conditioned by the fact that we can and do speak in a reasoned way, or do logos and understanding, politics is nevertheless based on a fundamental disturbance, a fundamental rupture or break of speaking. This is the basis of the second paradigm: politics based on a break in speaking. This is exactly the not speaking that I reference in this series' title: a break, a rupture, an impossibility; some kind of a problem of speaking, dis-communication. I will sometimes denote these things with

Introduction | 3

a term I coined, "logoclasm." You may have heard of iconoclasm, the term for different religious or philosophical trends that act against images, against idolatry. This often refers to people in monotheistic religions breaking statues or images of other gods. If iconoclasm denotes the breaking of images, logoclasm is the breaking of logos. It is a term for saying a lot of things, such as not talking, dis-communication, rupture, and so forth.

So the first paradigm is politics of speaking, and the second is politics of not speaking. If the first paradigm has Aristotle as a precursor, the second paradigm has a different precursor from a different textual tradition. It comes not from philosophy, but from what is sometimes called biblical mythology. The Tower of Babel is a very famous myth at the beginning of the Bible in which all of humanity comes together to build a city. It is about politics, the formation of politics, about building a *polis*, a tower, in which everyone cooperates. Everyone has one language, so they can work together quickly, but for some reason the God or gods—it is denoted in the plural—is unhappy with this project and divinely intervenes to disturb language. This one language that original humanity spoke becomes diverse, and this is how linguistic diversity was born. This is the mythological moment in which the split in language is created, but also the moment when different societies, religions, ethnicities, and political entities were created. In a sense, it is the beginning of politics. According to this myth, the beginning of the history of politics is when language is broken, communication interrupted: logoclasm. The myth of Babel tells of the foundation of politics as a break in language.

If for Aristotle politics is logos or language, the Tower of Babel describes politics as the breaking of language. Looking back on political history today, it is not surprising that central political events are less about people talking and more about people having communication problems and resorting to other means, especially violence. One can think about wars that are currently on the rise, violent struggles, and riots, but also nonviolent forms of not speaking, such as silencing or boycotting. These are all phenomena that are central to both political history and the political present. Clearly politics is often about not speaking; it is often about the failure of communication rather than about communication.

Of the two paradigms, politics as about speaking and politics as about not speaking, this seminar explores the second, namely politics as based on miscommunication. We do so by exploring five different thinkers who wrote five different texts in the twentieth century. They have various positions on politics as based on not speaking, as logoclasm. In addition, we talk

4 | Politics of Not Speaking

about how these texts communicate or miscommunicate. The journey is chronological insofar as we move from the oldest text to the most recent. We start with Carl Schmitt's text, written in the thirties, then move on to Martin Heidegger in the fifties, Frantz Fanon in the sixties, Gayatri Spivak in the eighties, and finally Jacques Derrida in the mid-nineties.

Two concepts, or notions, are central to all our readings. The first is difference. When I mentioned the Tower of Babel, I talked about the mythological beginning of politics as the splitting of humanity into different groups, civilizations, states, and so on. This question of politics and difference arises often in our discussions, whether in a cultural or religious context. Sometimes we talk about epistemic difference. *Episteme* is another Greek word that is used today to talk about systems of knowledge, that is, about how societies organize their knowledge and thinking through concepts and categories, but also institutions. Thus, I am talking not only about cultural difference, but also about the difference between systems of knowledge, or epistemic difference. If, in one society, for example, knowledge is organized around universities and university discourse, and in another society knowledge is organized around Islamic madrasas or Jewish yeshivot, then we can speak here about three different systems of knowledge.

The second concept, or notion, that is important throughout our discussion refers to a specific historical kind of politics of difference, the politics of colonialism and decolonialism. We will soon discuss what exactly these two words mean, but you have undoubtedly already heard of these categories. Today they are becoming more and more current, not only in academic and intellectual discourses, but also in cultural and broader ones. In this context, we will talk about colonial and postcolonial logo-politics, or how the question of politics and not speaking plays a role in the political-historical phenomena of colonialism, decolonialism, and postcolonialism. If you are following the news, you probably have already had a chance to see that we often encounter questions concerning the limits of speaking—what one is allowed or not allowed to say or speak and with whom—in the context of colonialism or postcolonialism. For example, in Germany, the documenta debate about anti-Semitism and postcolonialism recently revealed an entry point into the question of who is allowed to say what. In this context, art works or intellectuals from the Global South who suggested analogies between what Germany did to Jews and what Israel does to Palestinians broke a taboo in German discourse, were accused of anti-Semitism, and silenced.

Let us now turn to the texts.

1

Politics as Break of Logos: Carl Schmitt

The first text we will speak about, Carl Schmitt's *Der Begriff des Politischen*, *The Concept of the Political*, was first written in 1927, but the standard edition read today is from 1932.[1] In a sense, it is a continuation of an earlier text that Schmitt wrote in 1922, which is also very famous, *Politische Theologie*, *Political Theology*.[2] Schmitt was a legal scholar in Berlin working at Humboldt University, and he became a functionary in the early National Socialist state machinery. Like many German thinkers from the 1930s, Schmitt is a problematic figure. He has a huge influence on how we think about politics today. Schmitt had some notions that political theorists, whatever their political leanings, left or right, find helpful in many ways. Conversely, he made some dubious political decisions: at a certain point he joined forces and was intimately engaged with National Socialism. He is, in fact, considered one of the most prominent legal scholars in Germany to have cooperated to a significant extent with National Socialism. The dynamic regarding the debate over Schmitt's past is similar to that surrounding Martin Heidegger. Heidegger was an important philosopher who also had an influence on thinkers from left to right throughout the twentieth and twenty-first century. At a certain moment of his life, and in a very categoric way, he was a Nazi and never became anti-Nazi or dissident in any way. Both Schmitt and Heidegger are thus similarly problematic and influential.

I want to talk about Schmitt as a thinker of politics as a logoclastic domain, or a domain in which language, speaking, discourse, or logos breaks. He is the earliest thinker we discuss who could be described as a paradigmatic and exemplary thinker of politics of not speaking. One

6 | Politics of Not Speaking

concept that is important for Schmitt, and around which much of his thought revolves, is the concept of war as central to politics. I have already mentioned war as one of those events or phenomena that one associates with the political happening and that clearly mark a failure or collapse of speaking. For Schmitt, war, or conflict more generally, is indeed important for understanding politics. For Schmitt, politics is not about ending conflicts. It is not about creating a society without conflicts, and it is not about solving or abolishing a state of conflict; it is almost the opposite: politics is about existing within conflict. Conflict belongs to the essence of politics.

I begin with conflict, or even war, as what Schmitt understands as the very essence of political language. At a certain point, he says that political language is a language of conflict. It is a polemic language spoken in defiance of something. Schmitt writes that

> all political concepts, images, and terms have a polemical meaning. They are focused on a specific conflict and are bound to a concrete situation; the result (which manifests itself in war or revolution) is a friend-enemy grouping, and they turn into empty and ghostlike abstractions when this situation disappears. Words such as state, republic, society, class, as well as sovereignty, constitutional state, absolutism, dictatorship, economic planning, neutral or total state, and so on, are incomprehensible if one does not know exactly who is to be affected, combated, refuted, or negated by such a term. (30)

Schmitt is saying that when people started saying the word "state," it was a declaration of a war of sorts against someone else. Furthermore, we don't understand what state means anymore, because as a political concept it was originally a contestation of and opposition to something. Thus, political language is a language of polemics. He continues: "Above all the polemical character determines the use of the word political. The word political regardless of whether the adversary is designated as nonpolitical in the sense of harmless or vice versa if one wants to disqualify or denounce him as political in order to portray oneself as nonpolitical (in the sense of purely scientific, purely moral, purely juristic, purely aesthetic, purely economic, or on the basis of similar purities) and thereby superior" (32). Sometimes the word "political" is used to describe a position that is not objective. For instance, when in a debate someone says: "I am talking in the name of truth, and you are just being political." Schmitt argues that the word political is itself polemic. It is just an example of how all political language is polemic. In other words, the conflict is in political language itself.

There is another word, although Schmitt does not mention it, that is highly polemic in his political thought: *polemos*. Polemics comes from *polemos*, a Greek word that can be translated as war. It can also be translated as polemics, or the exercise of conflict in language. In Schmitt, we will see that there is a conflict about the true nature of political conflict, namely about whether it concerns polemics (arguments, discussions, and debates) or war. I argue that Schmitt sees the true nature of political conflict as war, and that he understands war precisely as different from polemics, which is characterized by logos, or speaking. He understands war as the break, the interruption of logos and speaking, or where *polemos* fails. It is for this reason that I aim to illustrate Schmitt as a paradigmatic thinker of politics as the failure of language, as the failure of speaking, or simply not speaking.

The best way to approach the heart of Schmitt's thought is to understand what his own polemics were. Against whom did Schmitt say what he had to say? He underlines politics as defined by conflict; there is no objective or neutral political theory. Political theory is always a contestation of some other ideas about politics. I suggest that Schmitt's basic critique is addressed toward a politics of antiwar, or a politics aimed at ending war. More provocatively put, this is a politics that declares war on war, or antiwar politics. One could use Schmitt to analyze a paradox whereby modernity philosophically understood itself in many ways as the age of reason, the age of understanding, the age of speaking, democracy; however, the same modernity also generated the most extreme forms of war in terms of scope, measure of destruction, and so forth. Thus, Schmitt can be used to examine this paradox about the meaning of modernity.

There are two forms of antiwar politics that Schmitt's thinking criticizes. One is what Schmitt calls liberalism, and the other is what he calls either anarchism or revolutionary politics. These are two different forms of modern antiwar politics, or politics aimed at ending war. Interestingly, these two forms are in conflict with each other, and this is Schmitt's point. First, it is important to define liberalism and anarchism or revolutionary politics in this context. For the sake of this discussion, one could define liberalism as a politics according to which the solution to end war is the modern, democratic state and its laws as a haven of peace. In contrast, according to Schmitt's analysis, anarchism or revolutionary politics is a kind of politics for which the solution to end war is the dissolution of the state. If liberalism

8 | Politics of Not Speaking

thinks that the state is the solution to combat war, anarchism thinks that the state is the problem and that, to live in peace, the state needs to be abolished. These two positions embody the ideas of peace as state and peace as anti-state; this is why they are in conflict.

Schmitt has two different ways of arguing or critiquing these two forms of antiwar politics. Schmitt makes a factual argument against liberalism. If liberalism thinks that the modern, sovereign state is based on peace, the end of war, Schmitt argues that the state is actually based on conflict. This can be framed in terms of speaking and logos. Schmitt criticizes political and legal theorists such as Hans Kelsen, an important name in legal theory in the twentieth century and an adversary of Schmitt. Schmitt criticized those who analyzed the state as based on the rule of law. Kelsen analyzed the existence of the state, namely our political system, as a system that is based on laws and a hierarchy of laws, a normative and logical system. There are different norms that interact with each other, and one could analyze and systematically reach various solutions to different problems; one could say that state law is some kind of logos, a kind of a perfect system of reasoning. Against these notions, or visions of understanding of what comprises the state and state law, Schmitt proposes a different understanding. This is underlined by one of his most famous statements, the first argument in *Political Theology*. Schmitt often opened his texts with a short and concise statement that would go on to become famous.

I will read it to you, first in German: "*Souverän ist wer über den Ausnahmezustand entscheidet.*" The sovereign is he who decides about the state of exception (*Ausnahmezustand*). This one short sentence is the core of Schmitt's critique of liberalism as an approach to the state as based on the rule of law. Schmitt argues that the state is based on sovereignty and that what is important to understand in our political systems, our states, is that they are sovereign. In this context, sovereignty denotes something that has absolute power and is not subject to any norm. Sovereign states are not committed to anything; no one can tell them as states what to do. One often hears about this or that head of state complaining about an intervention in their sovereignty. This means that the state decides for itself, and no one can tell it what to do. Schmitt says that sovereignty—the essence of a state, a system that is completely and absolutely autonomous—is not based on the rule of law. Quite the contrary, the sovereign of the state is the one who holds the power to declare an exception to the law. The state exists as it is because there is a sovereign who, at a certain moment, decides on an exception, to which the law no longer applies. Current examples include decisions regarding COVID-19 or wars. In a state of exception, the law no longer applies. What one thinks is the law, a beautiful system of logically interconnected norms, does not apply anymore.

Schmitt argues that the basic principles of the modern state are based on this power of the sovereign. This entails an exception—the state of exception—and a decision. The sovereign decides. "Decides" for Schmitt means that the sovereign does not just logically infer. There may be arguments made, a process of reasoning and convincing, but the final decision is not merely a deduction of a certain solution from a set of rules. The sovereign decides *"aus den Nichts,"* from nothing. There is no principle from which the sovereign deduces their ultimate decision. If the sovereign decides that we are now at a moment that requires the suspension of law, there can be no norm that determines this decision; it is an absolute decision. There is no logos, no reason, no discourse, that dictates the decision. This is Schmitt's critique of liberalism. Our states are not built on some kind of ideal state of reasoning, but rather the principle of sovereignty that is committed to no logic. Schmitt's critique of liberalism is a factual analysis based on his legal theoretical analysis of how modern law functions.

However, Schmitt also has another adversary. The second antiwar politics that Schmitt criticizes is anarchism or revolutionary politics. Anarchists agree with Schmitt's factual analysis that the state is not an ideal form of politics but rather a principle of absolute power. Anarchists want to dissolve the state to reach peace. Schmitt's argument here is no longer about the nature of the modern state or about politics, because he and the anarchists basically agree on this. Schmitt's argument concerns what he calls the nature of the human being. He asks how the human being is understood, and more precisely how human beings relate to goodness; the way we understand human nature will reflect how we understand politics. He argues that anarchists are motivated by the notion that human nature is essentially good. Accordingly, if all the obstacles were removed and people could behave naturally, then peace would reign. In contrast, Schmitt says that politics, historically and essentially, is based on the assumption that human nature is not good but actually evil.

In defining human nature as evil, Schmitt does not imply that people purposely harm others. He does not mean that humans want to be good but are somehow always tempted to do bad things. This is not his point. His point is that, historically, humans exist in a certain state in which they objectively are unable to achieve what they think is good, or they are unable to understand or reach a consensus about what is good. Therefore,

10 | Politics of Not Speaking

if everybody is committed to thinking about what is best for others and doing what is best for everybody, they will find themselves in wars of differing goods. The best example of this is the war between liberalism and anarchism: both sides think that they are doing what is best for everybody. Schmitt says that human nature is bad because following the concept of good in an unconditional way simply brings one into conflict with another attempt to do good.

For Schmitt, this understanding of human nature as evil is inherently connected to a political tradition. Schmitt understands the whole doctrine about the human as evil in connection to the Christian notion of original or hereditary sin. The idea of original or hereditary sin goes back to the beginning, to the origin of humanity, to the biblical myth of paradise before the Tower of Babel story. It refers to the story of Adam and Eve's beautiful existence in paradise and the prohibition of eating from the tree of knowledge. This is followed by the first sin: disobeying the prohibition by eating from the tree of knowledge, and subsequently falling from paradise. Paradise lost. According to this Christian doctrine, this fall marked the beginning of human history; and at the end of this history, there will be redemption from sin. At the end of history, a redeeming moment will bring humans back to this state of paradise. Schmitt refers to this idea of sin. He is Catholic and thinks that the theology of sin or theories like it are at the basis of politics. According to these theories, humanity is unable to find a shared good, and this is why it is essentially evil. Evil is not based on the will to do bad things, but rather stems from the fact that humans are unable to follow through with the good things that they want. Schmitt draws on this anthropological premise to critique anarchism or revolutionary politics.

Perhaps the most important part of Schmitt's argument is that as long as we are under the state of sin or evil, as long as we as humanity are objectively unable to achieve a common good, any attempt to try to end the evil state, any attempt to end war, will lead to the worst kind of war. This is one of the basic understandings of Schmitt, and still the most interesting today. Schmitt argues that the minute a party to a conflict understands itself as representing not just one side of the war, but the side that is against war and evil, it will start fighting the other side, not just as the other side of the specific war, but as embodying evil. This war will become a war against war itself in which one side assumes the role of good fighting evil. It will not just entail winning a war. Instead, the war becomes a war of destruction of the other side as evil. This generates what Schmitt calls *Vernichtungskrieg*,

Politics as Break of Logos: Carl Schmitt | 11

a war of annihilation and extermination, which will follow any situation in which good and evil rather than two sides of a conflict are represented in a war. Schmitt argues:

> If pacifist hostility toward war were so strong as to drive pacifists into a war against nonpacifists, in a war against war, that would prove that pacifism truly possesses political energy because it is sufficiently strong to group men according to friend and enemy. If, in fact, the will to abolish war is so strong that it no longer shuns war, then it has become a political motive, i.e., it affirms, even if only as an extreme possibility, war and even the reason for war. Presently this appears to be a peculiar way of justifying wars. The war is then considered to constitute the absolute last war of humanity. Such a war is necessarily unusually intense and inhuman because, by transcending the limits of the political framework, it simultaneously degrades the enemy into moral and other categories and is forced to make of him a monster that must not only be defeated but also utterly destroyed. (36)

This is what Schmitt describes as the consequence of not understanding what politics is about and thinking that it entails abolishing war and creating a state of perfect logos. One can still find this kind of notion today, for instance in how people speak about the current war that is being fought in Ukraine. One is forced to constantly consider whether descriptions of what is happening there encompass a war of evil against good. Schmittian thinking could help understand this type of reflection. Another historical example that Schmitt discusses in his later texts, and which we will unpack later, is a tendency of European, particularly Western, culture to understand its campaigns outside the West as done in the name of universal humanism against civilizations that are less than human. They thereby create patterns of violence that come close to what Schmitt is talking about when he speaks about wars of annihilation, wars that are fought not only to defend a certain interest but also to subjugate or even destroy the adversary. We will see that imperialism or colonialism can be analyzed in Schmittian terms. His own idea of politics is ultimately about "hedging" war, or hedged war, a term that denotes that international politics is not about solving wars but rather limiting them. This involves creating systems of power and norms that limit war and avoid wars of extermination.

12 | Politics of Not Speaking

Q: What is the role of technology in Schmitt's concept of war?

A: Technology plays different roles for Schmitt. On the one hand, it is a utopian manifestation of reason in which everything just becomes a technical question. But technology is also power. Schmitt references technology in his last book, the *Nomos der Erde*, in which he deals with the situation of postwar international law. He speaks about the possibility of using the advanced technology of long-distance air and sea weapons as connected to the abstract way in which adversaries understand themselves. Technology in this sense engenders the possibility of intervening militarily without the need for physical presence; it reinforces the idea of the different adversaries not representing their limited territorial limits but rather standing for some kind of universal principles.

In this context of unpacking Schmitt's polemics against antiwar politics, especially with liberalism, I suggest that he proposes a certain war or conflict on the nature of what political conflict entails. According to Schmitt, liberalism understands politics as based on conflict; however, the nature of this conflict is language. It is a conflict that is based on discourse, on speaking. Liberals understand political conflict as a conflict based on words. Schmitt speaks about how liberals talk about eternal conversation, dialogue, and discussion. On a more practical level, these kinds of discussions mean that politics takes place in areas governed by reason and argumentation, such as the spheres of economy or technology. Politics is about problems that humans have that need some kind of technological solution, and the ensuing debate is about the best kind of technological solution.

Q: But who determines what is the best argument?

A: This goes precisely in the direction of Schmitt's critique of liberalism. Schmitt argues that liberalism leads to a kind of neutralization of politics and the idea of the decision. There is no decision within liberalism; the best argument simply wins. Schmitt says that this is the neutralization, and thus the end, of politics. Against this understanding of politics as based on reason, discussion, and speaking, Schmitt suggests that politics is based on a conflict that is not made up of words. He asserts that the basic conflict or opposition in politics is not one of ideas or words, but rather "*seinsmäßig*," an opposition rooted in being, in existence. It is an existential opposition, or, to use a more philosophical word, an ontic opposition. In this understanding, basic political opposition is not just words, ideas, or arguments; it

Politics as Break of Logos: Carl Schmitt | 13

is an opposition of entities, of beings. It is a conflict in which one entity or being is driven toward the existential negation of another being. Concretely, this means that political conflict is a conflict based on the physical killing of the other side through war. This is how Schmitt understands war: a conflict in which each side aims to physically kill the other.

A small passage from *The Concept of the Political* is central to this idea. Schmitt writes that "Just as the term enemy, the word combat, too, is to be understood in its original existential sense" (33). Here Schmitt describes the nature of political conflict. He argues that political struggle, conflict, *Kampf*, should be understood in an existential sense. It does not mean competition; nor does it mean pure intellectual controversy or symbolic wrestling in which every human being is somehow always involved (in which their entire life is a struggle) and every human being is a symbolic combatant. He asserts that while we are undoubtedly in constant conflict with ourselves or others, this is not what political combat is about. Rather, the concepts of friend, enemy, and combat refer to the real possibility of physical killing. Political struggle is a question of life and death; it is the most extreme consequence of enmity, of being adversaries. It does not have to be common, normal, something ideal or desirable; but it must nevertheless remain a real possibility for as long as the concepts of the enemy and politics remain valid. Schmitt argues that while there is not necessarily an act of actually killing each other at the basis of political struggle, such struggle does have at least a possibility of turning into actual violence. This is what makes it political, according to his analysis.

It is important to note two points about Schmitt's understanding of the nature of political conflict as no longer logical but existential. The first dimension of this concerns epistemological consequences. Epistemology here refers to how one knows politics, conflict, and war. Schmitt makes an interesting point about political knowledge. He says that because politics is no longer about a logical but rather an existential conflict, there is no way to achieve an outside or objective picture of the conflict situation. An outsider does not know better than those inside the conflict. In fact, an outsider is no longer in this existential situation and no longer even knows about it. He argues: "Only the actual participants can correctly recognize, understand, and judge the concrete situation and settle the extreme case of conflict. Each participant is in a position to judge whether the adversary intends to negate his opponent's way of life and therefore must be repulsed or fought in order to preserve one's own form of existence" (27). Only within the situation can one know if they are threatened or not. It does not concern an objective

14 | Politics of Not Speaking

type of knowledge but rather a decision. Am I under threat or not? This also means that one experiences and encounters war not as a situation of war, but rather through what Schmitt calls the deadly adversary, namely the foe or the political enemy. Another of Schmitt's most famous sayings states, "The specific political distinction to which political actions and motives can be reduced is that between friend and enemy" (26). This entails existential conflict at the basis of politics: it is not a conflict between ideas but rather between two parties that basically, structurally, want to kill each other. Normally they do not reach this point, but friend and foe lean in this direction.

The second point is that, for Schmitt, politics is not just any domain in human life. It is not like life is divided into sections such as love, technology, culture, and sports, with an additional section for politics. For Schmitt, politics is something that defines the entirety of human being. I call this the logoclastic mode of being, a mode of being in which our logical capacities, our communication, discourse, and reasoning, break or are under a condition of interruption. One arrives at a mode of political being when a certain disagreement or conflict reaches a level of extreme intensity and becomes political in the sense that is no longer in words. At that moment, a political situation is created.

Schmitt states, "The distinction of friend and enemy denotes the utmost degree of intensity of a union or separation, of an association or dissociation" (26). We agree and disagree on many things, but at a certain moment of intensity, we become enemies and want to kill each other. This is politics. A few pages later, Schmitt underlines that "The political is the most intense and extreme antagonism, and every concrete antagonism becomes that much more political the closer it approaches the most extreme point, that of the friend-enemy grouping" (29). With Schmitt, politics is based on an existential conflict, namely war, and war is not simply different from or even the opposite of logic, disagreement in language, argument, and reasoning. Rather, war arises from logic, from logical argumentation and disagreements, whatever their contents may be. It arises in the moment in which the disagreement becomes existential. Schmitt says that this is when the contradiction is no longer in the domain of reason and speech but becomes existential, a conflict of not speaking. It is based on speaking, but at a certain moment speaking or logos comes to an end. There would be no war without such speaking, without the initial disagreement in logos. Without the break or collapse of the logical exchange, we would not reach war and be political according to Schmitt's understanding.

A related question is how the last idea I discussed with Schmitt resonates with something like the Tower of Babel, or politics as based on an irrecoverable or at least momentarily irreversible break of communication or logos. One must bear in mind that Schmitt's advocacy was based on a politics that was nevertheless dependent on territorial state sovereignty as capable of limiting war. This idea has not really proven itself as something that reduces war, but rather it becomes the goal of war. There is a strong critique of Schmitt's position, but it is nevertheless useful to think through Schmitt for our future discussions in this series via the idea of politics as the collapse of logic, of politics as based on logoclasm.

Q: Does Schmitt talk about the temporality of politics?

A: Although he does not explicitly say so, I think that one can make sense of what Schmitt is doing without theology by translating sin and evil into time. He problematizes the liberal order by saying it is an eternal, infinite conversation. This is not to position temporality as evil but to explain the same condition that the terms evil or sin were trying to describe in non-theological or existential terms through the idea of finitude.

Q: Does Schmitt understand this in a Heideggerian way?

A: There is a certain *Zeitgeist* for this kind of thinking, and you can find connections between Heidegger and Schmitt. For example, both refer to Kierkegaard, precisely concerning the point of the decision and the existential root of all the different arguments and doctrines made in authentic or genuine kinds of thinking.

Q: You said that Schmitt tries to define sovereignty by this absolute that neither refers to any norms nor derives decisions for any arguments but rather decides. Do you think he achieves this in his later political thought, especially *Nomos of the Earth*, that is based on law as fence and enclosures? He is very clear on this; he obviously wants this order, the fence of *nomos*, against anarchic forces. But we can think of migrants, we can think of all kinds of de-territorializing flows that try to spread beyond borders in a transversal way and work against particular identities that states tend to engender.

A: You are right that Schmitt's early critique of the idea of perfect law can be seen through the person of the sovereign who is outside the law. His later critique of the idea of perfect law refers to the outside that consists not of the sovereign, but other states' laws. In this regard, he says that law is originally connected to a specific land, namely to deny that law is an

16 | Politics of Not Speaking

abstract and universal concept. Politics is originally connected to a certain group that is divided from other groups, and the most concrete way of understanding this is through territory. Therefore, the world is made up of plural polities. As to the question of immigrants, you are right in pointing out, as a critique of Schmitt, how the particular and specific national-statist identity can become absolute, to the point of seeing all other identities, especially those without state, the refugees, as destructive evil.

2

Dialogue as Violence: Martin Heidegger

Today we continue our journey into the politics of not speaking. We have talked about the relation between politics and language, discourse, or speech. I talked about "logo-politics," and I presented two models that can be roughly identified in different intellectual traditions. One is politics with speech, logos; and the other is politics without speech, as a rupture or a break with logos, which I call logoclasm, or logoclastic politics.

Yesterday we dealt with Carl Schmitt. I discussed some basic ideas in Schmitt that frame him as a paradigmatic thinker of politics as the break or interruption of logos, and so as a logoclastic political thinker. I showed the ways in which the paradigmatic event of collapse of logos, namely war, is central to Schmitt's thinking. We talked about war and the relation between war as an existential conflict that is about being, about life and death, and polemics as conflict existing in words, in logos. We discussed how war is neither the opposite of reason nor the eruption of irrationality, but an extreme mode of discourse of logics, or logos, a disruptive mode but one that nevertheless arises in the realm of logos. The politics of not speaking is not simply the opposite of politics of speaking: it is a mode of it.

Today we will speak about another thinker, Martin Heidegger. Heidegger is a central reference for philosophers from the thirties or forties onward in France, the United Kingdom, the United States, and Germany. Like Schmitt, Heidegger is a controversial figure. At a certain moment he was enthusiastically involved with the National Socialist movement and state, and although he later distanced himself from this, he never really explained what had happened. While Heidegger was not completely silent about it,

18 | Politics of Not Speaking

many feel that he could, and should, have said more. A few years ago, some of his notebooks were published, *The Black Notebooks*, in which he made problematic statements about Jews. Many think that Heidegger has been shown to be anti-Semitic, at least in some moments, which made his involvement with National Socialism even more dire. He is thus a contested figure today more than ever, one who is nonetheless influential in many ways, which is especially interesting for the sake of our discussion on the politics of not speaking.

The trope of silence is central for biographical studies of Heidegger: his silence after the war, his not complete silence but relatively low level of expression about the years of the war and what it meant and means, and his silence regarding politics. Heidegger himself is some kind of a figure of a politics of silence. Beyond, or in addition to, this biographical point of view, his thinking itself deals centrally with the question of language rather than with the question of politics. Heidegger did not say a lot about politics per se, even when he was politically engaged with or, according to his own statements, opposed to National Socialists in the thirties and forties. Nevertheless, one could say that his work has been one of the central politicizing philosophies of the twentieth century in the sense that he is a thinker who turned the entire approach to philosophy from an abstract system of thinking (a list of debates, concepts, and ideas) to a specific tradition of thought that is identified with a specific cultural civilization and world, namely the West, or Europe.

Today, it is almost—almost—banal to say that philosophy is a Western or European tradition that is deeply connected to Europe's civilizational and political performances. One example is the connection of philosophy to one of the central political performances of European civilization, colonialism, which we speak about more in the next lecture. As I mentioned in my introduction, this issue can also be identified in Schmitt. Although Heidegger did not speak about colonialism or imperialism per se, his gesture of speaking, showing, and talking about philosophy as a specific, certain, identified civilizational performance was very influential for later thinkers who engaged in more concrete political terms with what this means. Heidegger remains a major reference for this kind of approach, including tropes such as the end of philosophy, what lies beyond philosophy, and thought beyond philosophy. These were terms that Heidegger often spoke about in the abstract, but that other thinkers tried to understand in more concrete geographical or temporal terms. Heidegger's more broadly known conception of thinking and philosophy and his engagement with the questions of language and logos makes him a valuable thinker for our journey. Today, I introduce and discuss a text wherein these questions of language and politics come together and the question of silence, or not speaking, is very central.

The text we will discuss today is called "Aus einem Gespräch von der Sprache—Zwischen einem Japaner und einem Fragenden."[1] In Peter Hertz's English translation, it is called "A Dialogue on Language between a Japanese and an Inquirer." This text was written in 1953, so twenty years later than Schmitt and what we discussed yesterday, and it was originally published in a collection of texts on language. It is not one of Heidegger's more discussed and read texts; even those dealing specifically with language tend to give it relatively less attention. However, scholars who deal with intercultural dialogue or intercultural relations, what is sometimes called intercultural philosophy, are an exception. These are thinkers who are concerned with issues connected to the possibility of acknowledging and negotiating the existence of different worlds of thinking, an area in which philosophy is only one possibility. In this context, this text from Heidegger is considered important. Many non-Western thinkers, especially those active in Indian or Chinese thought, often read this text in such a context. One could say that it is an important text for the question of difference that delves deeply into intercultural difference, or, as I call it, inter-epistemic difference, the difference between different systems of thought, thinking, and knowledge in the broadest sense of the terms.

I have brought this text into our conversation because it problematizes the notion of dialogue in a fundamental way. In our discussion of the politics of not speaking, we are concerned with an idea of the political that is based on a collapse, end, or interruption of dialogue. This text from Heidegger problematizes the concept of dialogue itself, together with a long series of categories that are today considered central to intercultural relations and intercultural politics, such as conversation and exchange. Heidegger problematizes and shows the difficulties, and even the danger in dialogue. Heidegger's text barely mentions politics per se; but if one understands politics as a performance in the domain of difference, then this is without doubt a political text. It critiques dialogue and conversation, logos, *dia*-logos; the logos being exchanged, the flow of logos. It critiques dialogue as dangerous and—resonating a little with Schmitt from yesterday—violent. It presents dialogue as a form of violence, logos as a form of violence.

This is interesting in regard to yesterday. On the one hand it seemed we had logos, debate, conversation, and conflict with words, while on the

20 | Politics of Not Speaking

other it seemed we had a collapse that creates, generates, or simply is, violence in the form of physical killing and existential conflict. Heidegger provides a different perspective on logos itself as violence, as itself generating, manifesting, or deploying intercultural violence. In terms of speaking, we can call this violence in language silencing. Violence does not have to be outside language, it can be within language. At least one of these forms can be called silencing. This involves language that asserts a form of speech or a way of giving expression or talking that is simultaneously a performance of silencing. Language, through the act of talking, can simultaneously silence voices. There is, of course, a dialectics of language itself, of logos: the very manifestation of communication can prevent or suppress communication.

I want to start with the idea of translation as an example of language that silences. Translation is a speech act that manifests or shows, but at the same time can also conceal. These dialectics of simultaneously showing and concealing resonate very deeply in Heidegger's thought. Showing is at the same time an act of hiding or concealing. A concrete example of this is the translation of the title of the text that we are concerned with here. "A Dialogue on Language" is a translation of the German title, "*Aus einem Gespräch von der Sprache.*" This translation is a language act that gives voice in English to this originally German text. However, those of you who understand German can see that there is a problem with the translation. "A dialogue on language" is an easily understandable title, whereas "*Aus einem Gespräch von der Sprache*" is a much vaguer expression. The main difficulty is "*von.*" It is not "*über Sprache,*" on language, but rather "*von der Sprache.*" It is not completely unintelligible, but it is challenging to see what exactly Heidegger means. "*Von*" could mean "of" or "from." "*Von*" could designate provenance, as in coming from somewhere, or it could signal the possessive, as in the ownership of a book. It creates a very strong relation between the *Gespräch* (the conversation or dialogue) and language, *Sprache* in the sense that the conversation somehow belongs to language.

This strong relationship is not apparent in the expression "a dialogue on language," which implies a more distant relation, a conversation that bears upon, addresses, concerns, language but does not necessarily belong to it in the same strong way. If you have read the text, you can see that this distinction becomes critical at a certain moment. In a sense, it is almost the essence of Heidegger's point: the relationship between speech and what is spoken of. The English version is mistranslated in this regard, yet those of you who translate will know that I'm not criticizing the translator. Translating is a very difficult matter, and every translation is also potentially a mistranslation. So this is not a critique of Peter Hertz, but rather an attempt to show this act of language as an example of dialogue or language that is simultaneously an act of silencing. The few moments in the text I want to discuss are moments that show how the act of conversation or dialogue is simultaneously an act of creating silence. This takes on various forms, including a violent kind of silence, or a silence that is corrective, or a silence that tries to avoid silencing. I use the concept of logoclasm that I introduced earlier to show how Heidegger's text itself performs the collapse of logos.

I want to show how Heidegger's text performs a dialogue that performs a collapse—I even go further and use the word "death"—of dialogue, logos that performs logoclasm. There is a certain death of language, or death of communication, from or of language in this dialogue. Two central features of this text already point in this direction, the first being its genre. It is a dialogue and not a linear treatise that simply talks about something, starts with an argument, and continues. Philosophical texts are usually not even monologues; there is usually no person speaking. We know that there is an author who sometimes says "I" in the text, but the text itself does not include a person speaking. There are some famous monologues, in which a person speaks, for example, Hamlet, but in most philosophical texts there is not even this. Kant is on the cover of the book, but Kant is not a person in the text. It is simply an impersonal flow of logos; even if one says "I," it is not attributed to a person. It is a transcendental I. A dialogue, or even a monologue, is a different situation in which the text itself already contains an extra-logic entity. A dialogue illustrates this even in the graphic layout of the text: there is the name of someone, there is their designation, and then comes language. One can say that this is part of the text, but as part of the text at the same time it contains an element that goes outside the text.

Imagine a conversation in which the speakers don't say "I, Heidegger" or "I, Socrates," but just speak. If one were present at this exchange, this would just be voices, but as a written text it has signs that tell us that it contains something outside of language. I see this as a kind of logoclastic element in the very staging of a dialogue. This does not mean staging in the sense of performing onstage, but in the sense of presenting an argument or some kind of speech as a dialogue in a text. The words are already attributed to something that is no longer just words: it is a speaking entity, a person. They are attributed to something that is no longer just a logical component. The dramatic element in all dialogues, not just Heidegger's, includes some kind of a moment in which logos breaks. Logos is not just floating in the air like arguments or ideas, but somehow has a beginning and an end and

22 | Politics of Not Speaking

is both marked with words and no longer just words. Of course, I am not speaking about the actual Heidegger and Japanese philosopher in this text, but about names or designations as beginning and end of logos.

The second feature that breaks conversation or logos in the text via its performance is the specific speaking entities, the Japanese and the Inquirer, *der Fragende*. These designations represent different cultures, a word ("culture") that Heidegger does not use, and in fact hates, but which is suitable for our purposes. The text concerns an encounter between different cultures, different epistemes, namely different systems of thought and their categories of understanding the world. It deals with different beings, or being-theres ("being-there" is Heidegger's word for a human being, *Dasein*), different houses of beings, or, as Heidegger sometimes says in this text, "*Sprachgeist*," or the spirit of language. It presents different worlds, different civilizations. One of these is European, the other East Asian, and while the text never identifies the European culture as German, the East Asian culture is identified as Japanese. Furthermore, the European speaker is not identified as German, although he is (Heidegger, the Inquirer), while the other speaker is clearly identified as Japanese.

The Japanese is probably based on a real encounter that Heidegger had with a Japanese intellectual named Tomio Tezuka, who visited him in the fifties. As we learn in the text, Tezuka was a student of a Japanese philosopher, Count Shuzo Kuki, who had visited Heidegger in the twenties and thirties. There is scholarship dealing with the relationship between Heidegger and Japanese or non-Western thinkers. Heidegger had a huge influence on non-Western cultures in the process of these cultures understanding themselves as non-Western and different. He experienced a very strong reception in Japan, China, and the Islamic world, especially in Iran, and also among Jewish thinkers. Heidegger thus had a large influence outside the West for the non-West to understand itself as such, but Japan is one of the first and most significant places.

It is important to also think critically about these texts, first, about the specific kind of otherness or cultural difference with which these texts engage the European. There is a long German tradition stretching back to the eighteenth century rooted in a fascination with East Asian, Chinese, Japanese, and Indian cultures in parallel with a negative fascination with West Asian, Semitic cultures. There is a whole tradition, also connected to theology, that aspires to find some kind of kinship between German Nordic European, even Christian, culture and a past that does not lie in the Semitic, Mesopotamian world, but rather in East Asia, an Arian connection. Thus,

Heidegger's choosing to have an intercultural encounter in 1953 with an East Asian figure is not insignificant. A second critical aspect of this text is that, although this is an intercultural encounter, the Asian, the Japanese is marked as such, whereas the European, German is not, but rather as *Fragende*, Inquirer. This second figure has no cultural attribution, but is designated as an agent of logos, someone who is a seeker, who asks a question. There is an asymmetry in this relationship, which is not necessarily problematic, but is significant.

To engage with this exchange or encounter between two different cultures, I offer a theatrical reading of the text. I want to take the staging of this logos seriously; I frame it as an encounter, not only between words but also, to quote Schmitt, as an encounter between existential beings. I want to consider this conversation as a happening, as something that takes place. Furthermore, I suggest that one can see this text as a play in two acts in which the central performance is the death of logos, which stems from the death of dialogue in the middle of the first act. This death of dialogue permeates the text from the very beginning, whereas the second act offers something like—the theological undertone is not coincidental—a resurrection of dialogue: a death and resurrection of logos. Again, theology is important in the text and becomes manifest in a few important moments. Thinking back to Schmitt, theology also plays an important role, especially in our previous discussion on his thoughts on sin and political theology.

I start the play by reading one passage that I think encapsulates this idea of death and resurrection and offers some kind of a messianic, even eschatological, tone that I will soon make explicit. In this passage, Heidegger expresses a vision of the horizon that he looks toward in this problematic encounter between two different cultures, languages, and systems of knowledge. It is an encounter in which there is a disruption, even a death, of dialogue. Heidegger begins this passage by doubting his ability to grasp "the nature of the Eastasian language" (8). He then says something that I want to read more slowly as a kind of voice that goes through the dialogue and encapsulates its essence. Heidegger is now evoking the possibility of a certain end, a telos, a horizon toward which the efforts in the dialogue are directed: "Whether in the end—which would also be a beginning—a nature of language can also reach the thinking experience, a nature or essence that would offer the assurance that European-Western saying and Eastasian saying will enter into dialogue such that in it there sings something that wells up from a single source" (8). There are a lot of metaphors and images in this passage, which refers to a conversation in which two voices might

24 | Politics of Not Speaking

ultimately converge to create a song that springs from a single source, a certain eschatology of unity. This is what I call Heidegger's eschatological vision. Again, eschatology is a certain logos that relates to the *eschaton*, the last thing, or "the end" in Greek. It is a very important theological genre that refers to the apocalyptic or messianic. A sentence from the Bible resonates very strongly with Heidegger's words here, a sentence from a verse in which one of the minor prophets, Zephaniah, describes the messianic or end times in an uplifting way in terms of language. At the end of times, "I will purify the lips of the people that all of them may call on the name of Jehovah and serve him shoulder to shoulder" (Zephaniah 3:9). It is a logic-linguistic eschatology that resonates strongly with the Tower of Babel. As we have discussed, this story begins with everyone speaking the same language, but then there is a break, a split, followed by diverse languages and peoples. Zephaniah gives a vision of the end of time and redemption that goes back to language, the idea that everyone will speak the same language and use the same name. I suggest that Heidegger proposes a similar vision, one in which different cultures speaking different languages nonetheless look toward a horizon in which there is a moment of convergence and harmony, where all sing together from one source. Act One: death; Act Two: resurrection, led by this eschatology.

I now present these two acts: death and resurrection. The whole dialogue, the whole conversation, begins with death. It begins with a reflection, memory, commemoration, *Andenken*, concerning an earlier encounter, an earlier *Gespräch*, an earlier dialogue, between Europe and Japan. It involves Heidegger himself and the aforementioned Count Shuzo Kuki, who visited Heidegger in 1927. He was one of the first scholars ever to deal with Heidegger's work, and it was he who introduced him to Japan. The dialogue begins with reminiscing about this earlier encounter upon the occasion of Kuki's death. It begins with a reflection on Kuki's grave in Kyoto, which I see as symbolizing the death of the encounter between Heidegger and Kuki. Kuki represents a kind of encounter that took place, and the dialogue begins with the death of that. A dramatic end.

What was this earlier dialogue between Kuki and Heidegger? The reader is told that it was centered around Kuki's attempt to conceptualize an understanding of Japanese art that has its essence in the Japanese term *Iki*. He wanted to understand this Japanese aesthetics or art through European-Western discussions about aesthetics. Shortly after the symbol of Kuki's death, Heidegger reflects back on his relationship with Kuki and strongly criticizes their encounter, this intercultural dialogue, as a failure. He looks back and contemplates not only the physical death of Kuki, but how the previous dialogue itself had already committed a certain kind of violence and brought about death.

What is this problem that Heidegger addresses? Writing in the 1950s, Heidegger looks back on his encounter with a Japanese philosopher in the 1920s or 1930s. He is very critical about the possibilities that could arise from the type of dialogue that took place. This goes to the heart of our conversation about not speaking and the problematics of conversation. Heidegger speaks about a certain inter-dialogue, an intercultural conversation, that is almost, if not completely, impossible because of the nature of language. For Heidegger, language is not just a system of signs to designate entities that exist outside language, or different arbitrary names that could use German or French or Japanese signs and remain the same. Heidegger asserts that language is our system of concepts, categories, and basic notions through which we not only see, but also construct the world. The things we experience in the world as objects are already, in their very essence, arising from and connected to language.

A world is somehow framed and shaped by language. The expression that Heidegger uses in the text, but had actually coined a few years earlier in his famous "Letter on Humanism," is that language is the house of being, *des Haus des Seins*. It is an interesting metaphor that he does not really explain, but I think it helps one imagine a certain shape, structure, or space that language provides so as to domesticate or cultivate existence. Think of the Tower of Babel. Just as there are different architectures that shape our physical environments, so too is there a cultural, epistemic architecture that is perhaps even more fundamental to defining basic ways of approaching the world. Thus, Heidegger understands the idea of language as based on different languages creating, generating, and belonging to different worlds in fundamental ways. This is the basis of why he sees communication between two different languages as a very difficult task. It does not just entail converting one system of signs to another, but rather the need for communication between two very different ways of understanding reality.

At a certain point he says very clearly that "a dialogue from house to house remains nearly impossible" (5). Not completely, but nearly. When Heidegger says that language is the house of being, he means that different languages are not simply different systems of signs. French and English have different systems of signs, but not necessarily different houses. He rather speaks here about Europe and East Asia, specifically German and Japanese systems of signs. It is not just about the semantic identity of a certain

26 | Politics of Not Speaking

system of signs, but the basic categories of thinking about or experiencing the world. There is a failure, a necessary structural failure, impossibility, of logos, *dia*-logos, that is in a sense essential to the very existence of different cultures, of different languages. We return to Babel once again.

In this context, what was the problem with the conversation with Kuki and his attempt to understand Japanese art, *Iki*, through European aesthetics? Heidegger says that European aesthetics and Japanese art are very different. He asserts that European language—and once again, it is not important if it is German, English, or French, but rather European language or the set of categories and basic concepts through which Europe understands the world—has a certain character. There is a basic way in which European languages and peoples understand the world. Heidegger does not designate this as an individual phenomenon, but rather as a cultural tendency, a certain way of understanding the world that is different from an East Asian conceptualization. This relates back to my previous point about Heidegger treating philosophy as a cultural product.

The way that Heidegger identifies or describes European language or philosophy is well-known: he describes it as based in metaphysics, or a metaphysical way of understanding the world. This notion is something that he uses over and over again. What exactly this means changes, but one important feature for the text in question is that metaphysics is based on a difference between the physical, the bodily, the material, the real, and something beyond this: the metaphysical. This something is not body but soul, not reality but ideas, not being but thinking. According to Heidegger, this difference between the physical and the metaphysical, this separation, is a major feature of metaphysics. According to him, European language, or ways of understanding language, is also based on a metaphysical separation between material sign (a letter, a certain kind of voice or a phonetic structure) and some idea or object signified through the sign. In this schema, there exist the word and the idea, which are separate.

In this text, Heidegger argues that the specific nature of Western European language makes it nearly impossible to conduct the type of dialogue that Kuki was attempting to enact, namely to explain Japanese ideas, notions, or realities—in this case art—with European categories. This involves two different worlds, and Heidegger argues that this task is not just—nearly—impossible, but dangerous. Now comes the dramatic, tragic if you wish, part. Heidegger speaks about a deadly danger lurking in Kuki's aforementioned attempt to give voice to Japanese art via European words and ideas. Heidegger argues that this kind of attempt is dangerous because it creates language that silences. Earlier, I talked about dialogues that are actually a kind of violent silencing, and Heidegger asserts that this is precisely what Kuki enacted. Kuki was trying to explain, understand, Japanese art. By using European language, he created a certain expression of Japanese art that in reality silenced Japanese art. He created the appearance of giving words to Japanese aesthetics, but at the same time he concealed Japanese aesthetics by showing something as Japanese aesthetics that was actually European ideas. Thus, a dialogue brought death in the sense of silence.

"The language of the dialogue constantly destroyed the possibility of saying what the dialogue was about" (5). This is the paradoxical point: the very language of the dialogue, the common language that enabled it, destroyed the possibility of saying what the dialogue was about, namely Japanese art. The language was European; the dialogue was about Japanese art. Thus, through the very act of saying or expressing it, it paradoxically became impossible to say it. On the next page, Heidegger says that "the danger of our dialogues," namely his and Kuki's earlier dialogues, "was hidden in language itself" (4). The danger was in the language, "not in *what* we discussed, nor in the *way in which* we tried to do so," but in language itself. Neither the content of nor the specific method that they both chose to speak, but the very language they used, namely European, German language.

This death that Heidegger describes—the failure of dialogue by the performance of dialogue, the act of silencing through speaking—is not only a theoretical, philosophical question. It does not only concern whether we understand the nature of Japanese art. This is the moment when the text becomes more political, when Heidegger speaks about European colonialism. He sees the encounter between the Japanese philosopher and the German philosopher as just one performance within a broader context of the encounter between the West and the non-West in which there is no symmetry, but rather an encounter of power. Heidegger reflects upon how his encounter with a Japanese philosopher both concealed Japanese art and reflected a broader phenomenon in which Europe takes over what is outside Europe. He calls it the Europeanization of the globe, namely the imperial expansion of European culture and power to take over and enter into conversation with other cultures in which these cultures do receive some kind of language—do receive universities and education systems, and are being colonized and educated—but this education and colonization come about by the European voice silencing non-European cultures and worlds.

This is a way of understanding colonization. It is not simple destruction. There are ways of simply killing people, but there is another way of not

28 | Politics of Not Speaking

simply killing but taking over the language and consciousness of a culture. This is what Heidegger is talking about. He also calls it technologization, namely the spreading, not of abstract ideas, but of a way of being in the world, namely the technological way. There is also a cinematic moment in the text in which Heidegger presents the film *Rashomon*, a classic Japanese film from the fifties, as an example of an authentic Japanese aesthetics. Yet his Japanese interlocutor warns him that there is a danger in this film. It gives you the sense of coming close to Japanese reality, but it does so in a European form, namely through a European form of technology, which from the very beginning frames the entire visuality, existence, phenomenality of what one sees. This aesthetic experience is similar to language in that both are spaces in which things can show themselves, ideas can be expressed, but through a particular enactment, which also entails some form of concealment.

I am coming to the close of the first act. It announces not only the end of dialogue, but dialogue itself as an end of communication. The dialogue ends in a tragic way, rendered impossible by the very act of language. One can reflect on how this is connected to yesterday's discussion of Schmitt's *Vernichtungskrieg*, the war of extermination. This idea concerns European colonization as something that destroys, kills its enemy as non-human, whereas Heidegger speaks about a more complex phenomenon in which the others of the West are not simply annihilated physically; they are re-worlded. This entails new enactments of languages, often understood as progress or development for non-European peoples and sometimes giving them new ways of reflecting upon or documenting their own cultures, but also bringing death to these non-European cultures. This involves logos as violence.

Now we come to the climax of Act One, where speaking stops. The moment in question takes place after Heidegger sheds such a dramatic problematic light on his earlier dialogue with Kuki, but nonetheless almost lures the new Japanese interlocutor into a new dialogue by asking him a question that sounds very much like the one originally posed to him by Kuki. Whereas Kuki asked Heidegger about the nature of European aesthetics to understand Japanese art, Heidegger asks the Japanese interlocutor about the essence of Japanese language. At a certain moment, he asks the Japanese for a word or expression for how one identifies, marks, refers to, speaks about what is called *Sprache*, "language," in German. In that moment, the dialogue theatrically falls into silence:

I: What does the Japanese world understand by language? Asked still more cautiously: Do you have in your language a word for what we call language? If not, how do you experience what with us is called language?

J: No one has ever asked me that question. And it seems to me also that we in our own Japanese world pay no heed to what you are asking me now. I must beg you, then, to allow me a few moments of reflection. (23)

This statement is followed by silence. In the text, the description of this silence is in parentheses and in a different font that no longer conveys a language spoken by the characters but rather takes a distant point of view that describes something that happens in silence: *The Japanese closes his eyes, lowers his head, and sinks into a long reflection. The Inquirer waits until his guest resumes the conversation*" (23). This is unusual in a philosophical text because the form of the dialogue is itself unusual. One does not find this kind of stage direction in Platonian dialogues. It is usually used in the context of theater to describe what the characters are doing onstage when they are not talking. This is a kind of language that speaks silence.

There is a kind of language that is a language of not speaking in the sense that it describes moments of silence. It intervenes in spoken language, in dialogue, but it marks an interruption of dialogue. This is why I call it the moment of silence. The entire drama of Act One, the death of the dialogue, comes to a place where the Japanese interlocutor faces the danger, also political, of what he is asked to do, namely, to produce a Japanese essence of language in European words. He hesitates and falls into silence. The text produces a moment of intercultural silence through Heidegger's self-critique of his earlier conversation. Now we come to Act Two. But first, a moment of silence.

Q: What do you make of the moments of shared silence? In the dramaturgy of the text, the first thing that struck me was that there is a moment in which three dots are used to refer to the characters silencing themselves. I see it as having import that goes beyond a rhetorical device to play a structural role in the text. It is a very unusual way of speaking, but I think it's actually what gives the dialogue energy. The silence works, oddly enough. Is the *Gespräch* a success or not? It is not asserted directly,

30 | Politics of Not Speaking

but is rather experienced through this shared silence. I worked a lot to try to reconstruct this text, taking those moments as structural points or queues for inflection, but I almost went mad, so I stopped.

A: The question of the three dots is important. In Act Two, I will claim that these three dots are not shared silences but mark a song. I will call them a song. The three dots are the eschatological moment, the eschatological event. We will get to that soon.

Curtain down, curtain up, Act Two: resurrection. Now there is a certain salvation, a redemption; or, as the text says at a certain moment, a saving word, a solving word, a *lösendes* word. After his interlocutor falls into silence, after the dialogue is interrupted, Heidegger nevertheless offers his interlocutor something that the interlocutor understands as a *lösendes Wort*, a solving or salvaging word, a kind of logical redemption. The word he offers is *Wink* in German, which is translated in the text as "hint." However, I think that it is better translated as a "nod" or a "hinting gesture"; it is hinting at something through a gesture. This *Wink* performs a gesture using a hand, a head. It is a speechless kind of speaking, speaking without words. Heidegger offers his interlocutor the idea of speaking without words, *Gebärde*, gesture. There are four gestures Heidegger performs in an attempt to resurrect the dialogue in a new mode of speechless saying.

The first of these *Winke* is the question itself. After Heidegger works so hard to show how dangerous, disastrous, and destructive his earlier dialogue with a Japanese philosopher had been, the fact that he even asks about how his interlocutor uses language already shows that he knows there is another way. He could just remain silent and say, "you know, we don't have much to say to each other at this point." But he doesn't. He prompts the interlocutor to nevertheless say something. This is the first gesture.

The second gesture is a switch in roles that Heidegger offers his interlocutor. He, the Inquirer, first offers a question that the Japanese feels unable to answer. Heidegger then reverses the conversation and offers to be the respondent. He is no longer just an inquirer, he is now the respondent to a more original question. He focuses on a question that, according to Heidegger, was originally asked by Kuki, who apparently had an entire conversation with Heidegger that was doomed to fail because it was destructive. Yet the text reveals that Kuki had a more original question when he came to Heidegger, one that did not only concern explaining Japanese art with Western metaphysics. Heidegger evokes a more original conversation that had taken place and in this sense rehabilitates, resurrects, the earlier exchange with Kuki. Heidegger says that the original question was not about Japanese art, but about hermeneutics. Heidegger retells the story and says that the original impetus for this exchange had actually been the Japanese thinker's desire to understand the nature of European hermeneutics. Heidegger says that his former Japanese interlocutor had been interested in European hermeneutics because he was interested in the essence of European language. Whereas Heidegger was interested in the essence of Japanese language, an interest that brought his current Japanese interlocutor to silence, Heidegger now says that the entire exchange had originally been prompted by a Japanese interest in European language. Thus, there is already a harmony between these two questions, questions that in a sense sought one another out over a period of twenty or thirty years. Both cultures ask each other the same question. This is Heidegger's second gesture.

The third gesture is what Heidegger says about hermeneutics itself. Heidegger proposes that hermeneutics is a Western European theological concept that nevertheless goes beyond the metaphysical separation between words and things, between physical and metaphysical. Heidegger says that, in hermeneutics, there is an understanding that the word becomes flesh. All your theological phantasies are invited here to explain "word becomes flesh," namely incarnation. Word and flesh, thinking and being, language and things, actually belong together. There is an obvious irony of a Christianity beyond metaphysics, but that is a separate matter. Heidegger uses hermeneutics to suggest that in Europe itself, in the West, there is also a trace of a non-metaphysical language that is not separated from being. A language that is not based on signs, namely physical objects that arbitrarily refer to metaphysical ideas, but a language that functions in a different way, namely through gestures. A language of *Wink*; not signs, not *Zeichnen*, but *Wink*.

The most concrete demonstration of this kind of language of European hermeneutics is given through the example of Japanese *Noh* theater, a type of theater based on gestures. To exemplify this theater, the text again falls into silence. The Japanese interlocutor demonstrates a *Noh* theater gesture, and we get another stage direction: "*The Japanese raises and holds his hands as described*" (18), a gesture that is supposed to hint, nod, gesture toward a mountain. The text doesn't say mountain, nor does it provide a picture of a mountain, but the actor makes a gesture that suggests or invokes a mountain. This is, ironically or interestingly, the way in which we understand

32 | Politics of Not Speaking

hermeneutics. Hermeneutics is a European trace of non-metaphysical language, a language of gestures, that can be exemplified by Japanese art. This is the third gesture, literally, that Heidegger makes toward his interlocutor to bring about the resurrection of logos.

The fourth gesture is when Heidegger tries to provide an understanding of the essence of language (or how best to come close to this) that is no longer metaphysics. It is not a language that speaks about things; it is not language that is a dialogue "on" language (where there is language on one side and things on the other); rather it is a language that operates through conversations "from" things. The speaking and the being to which the speaking refers belong together. It is a language whose existence is not abstract but manifests itself in gestures of language, namely in what Heidegger calls *Gespräch*. *Gespräch* is not only a sign for dialogue, it also means something like the performance of *Sprache*. Heidegger often uses the "ge" prefix at the beginning of nouns: *Gerede, Gespräch, Gebrach, Geschichte, Gestell*. There are a lot of Heideggerian terms referring to a reality of things that are generated through a verb. *Gestell* is from *stellen*, *Geschichte* from *schicken* or *geschehen*, and *Gespräch* is the manifestation of *sprechen*. Heidegger is speaking about *Gespräch* as the manifestation of this non-metaphysical way of speaking.

At the end of the text, the Japanese interlocutor accordingly regains confidence and dares to say how Japanese people designate language: he uses the Japanese word for language, *Koto ba*. Through this word, coming at the end of the text, the resurrection of the dialogue brings about an eschatological end of Heidegger's vision. I read this vision once again: "Whether in the end—which would also be a beginning—a nature of language can also reach the thinking experience. A nature or essence that would offer the assurance that European-Western saying and East Asian saying will enter into dialogue such that in it there sings something that wells up from a single source" (8). This vision is materialized at the end of this dialogue. The materialization is this coherence between the nature of language as such, the traces of this non-metaphysical language in Western hermeneutics, and the Japanese *Koto ba*, as Heidegger explains it. And so the very last exchange becomes basically a monologue that is divided between the two speakers and is simply continued through the three dots.

J: How are we to think that?

I: As the gathering of what endures . . .

Dialogue as Violence: Martin Heidegger | 33

J: . . . which, as you said recently, endures as what grants endurance. . .

I: . . . and stays the Same as the message. . .

J: . . . which needs us as messengers. (54)

How is one to think of this as the gathering of what endures between the three dots, endurance between the three dots, and what stays the same? It is basically one statement that is being divided between two voices in a more or less arbitrary way. You could listen to it as singing together from one source. Curtain down. Happy ending.

[Clapping]

That is the end of the dialogue, but not the end of what I have to say. This text shows acute understanding of the problematics of dialogue in an intercultural scene and as a political event of colonialism. But there is here at the end a moment of overcoming that problematic in a way that for me seems too fast. The story of death and resurrection is in many ways a reenactment of Europe, of Christianity, of a kind of linguistic messianism that nevertheless gives a happy ending that is almost pathetic. There are a lot of problems with this conversation. Nevertheless, I extract this idea of a conversation of silence from it. I now leave you with the question of what political vision is being articulated in this moment of a conversation of silence.

3

Decolonialism as Logoclasm: Frantz Fanon

First I presented Carl Schmitt as a paradigmatic twentieth-century thinker of politics as a break in dialogue or conversation, what I call logoclasm, or a break of logos. I argued that, in a sense, Schmitt understands the entire realm of politics as based on some logoclastic moment or principle. This arises from his understanding of the break of language as a certain extreme level of intensity, conflict, or disagreement, namely the level at which the conflict becomes existential and disagreement violent. For Schmitt, war lies at the heart of politics. I made the case that Schmitt, notwithstanding the problems connected to him, presents some aspects that are and have been useful for other thinkers. This concerns thinking through the difference and otherness at the heart of politics and ways in which there is a disturbance of communication of the pure flow of argumentation and reason in politics.

Yesterday, we focused on another controversial thinker, Martin Heidegger. We discussed his conversation on—or more precisely from or of—language, *Gespräch von der Sprache*, which I framed as a performance, a theatrical play. I argued that it not only speaks on or from rupture or disruption of language and logos, but the death of logos also serves as a complex, ambivalent event in which, within the scene of difference (namely the staging of an encounter between different cultures and civilizations), dialogue and conversation hold less of a promise and more of a danger of death, or, in the realm of language, a kind of silence. Heidegger presents dialogue itself as a form of silence and violence. At a certain moment, this conversation, dialogue—this performance, this conceptual, theoretical analysis and performance of intercultural dialogue as a form of silence or

36 | Politics of Not Speaking

violent silencing—also makes a more explicit reference to a historical political situation.

At a certain moment it is no longer bound to a philosophical exchange between an individual German European thinker—the Inquirer, Heidegger himself—and a Japanese philosopher. It rather becomes a question about the relations between the West or Europe and a non-European world within a very concrete historical violence and silencing, which the text calls Europeanization. I connect this global Europeanization and technologization to the category of colonialization. Heidegger doesn't use this term, but he nevertheless refers to these descriptions. The text thus involves a conversation between Europe and the rest of the world, in which the political effects of this kind of conversation are much more pernicious than we tend to think in terms of dialogue and intercultural exchange. It involves a certain type of communication, a certain language, a certain reasoning, that creates conversations and education, but at the same time carries within it silencing, concealment, death of the non-European culture.

The dialogue conversely offers a resurrection, promise, eschatology of a redemption from this situation of rupture, break, and political violence. Heidegger proposes the solution of non-metaphysical language of gesture. The text arrives surprisingly quickly at this more harmonious situation of different cultures and languages that do in fact reach an understanding about the nature of language. In this moment, Heidegger's eschatological vision at the end of the text is realized: the harmonious song in the languages of the two interlocutors, the two cultures, arrives at a nonetheless continuous logos in which one speaker continues the sentence of the other. I also offered a critical reflection about this theological moment of redemption; it comes too quickly and reenacts precisely the problems that Heidegger's critique of European culture warns against. This whole discussion circles around the issue of dialogue or conversation itself as a form of violence on a philosophical level, but also on a historical-political level. I used the word "colonialism," which was also one of the categories toward which I gestured at the very beginning as a site in which the politics of speaking or politics of not speaking becomes a concrete question rather than a purely philosophical one.

Today we will discuss a thinker who is very explicitly a figure of the discourse on colonialism and decolonialization, Frantz Fanon. He is one of the early thinkers of decolonialization both as theory and as performative political thought beyond theory and on the level of action. Today he is considered a theorist of postcolonial or decolonial thought. At the time he was writing, it was less clear, but in retrospect, he is one of the founding figures of this discourse and has laid down fundamental categories and ideas that are still used today. Fanon's ideas are crucial not only on the level of theory, but also on the level of actual politics that take place within movements that understand themselves as being part of decolonial dynamics.

Fanon came from Martinique, where he studied psychiatry and was trained as a psychiatrist. He worked in North Africa and then joined the National Liberation Front (the Algerian liberation movement) and became their theoretician. He formulated some basic thoughts, notions, categories, even strategies, of the decolonial struggle in real time during the Algerian war of Independence itself, which then inspired other struggles in other places that understood themselves as standing in the same tradition or situation. The Palestinian liberation movement and the Black Panthers were both influenced by Fanon. Many Fanonian ideas can be recognized in both their texts and forms of action. Thus, Fanon is a founding figure not only for decolonial theory, but also for decolonial practice. Today I will talk about one of Fanon's famous works, *Les Damnés de la Terre*, translated into English as *The Wretched of the Earth*.[1] As discussed yesterday, translation can lend a voice to something in another language while simultaneously silencing or concealing. *The Wretched of the Earth* conceals an important moment in Fanon's thought, *Les Damnés*, the damned. There are certain theological aspects that I think are lost in the translation of the word "wretched." We will get to this soon.

The Wretched of the Earth was published in 1961 and quickly gained impact, in part because it was prefaced by Jean Paul Sartre, who was then a very well-known philosopher who also engaged with decolonization. Like all of Fanon's books, it is a collection of texts. I focus on the first of these, "De la violence," "Concerning Violence." I want to explore how Fanon's thought shapes the decolonial discourse by locating a moment of logoclastic violence at the center of colonization, and therefore also within decolonialization. This violence is based on the collapse of logos, which is similar in essence to what we saw in the discussions on Heidegger and Schmitt. It forms a conceptual center around which many of Fanon's notions and ideas can be understood. In a sense, it gives a certain direction to the postcolonial or decolonial endeavor.

The heart of the matter concerns Fanon's understanding of colonialism. Heidegger focuses on a constellation of reality, world, and civilization, which he calls metaphysics and which he tries to understand, problematize, and go beyond. Fanon speaks in a similar way about colonialism, namely as a comprehensive, civilizational mode of existence. The heart of the matter concerns defining colonialism as a phenomenon. On a basic level, it is a historical-political phenomenon of mainly European powers going beyond Europe into non-European places and cultures and performing various forms of violence. This involves conquering, namely colonizing in the form of settling down, building colonies, economic exploitation, sheer physical annihilation, and so forth. While all of this is, of course, what is understood as colonization, there remains the question—again thinking of Heidegger—of the essence of this set of different political phenomena, the question of whether they can be understood as something that has one name, some guiding or common principle, through which different things that happen in different times and places can be understood. Fanon tries to understand colonialism in this manner. While he speaks about things that take place in specific places (the French colonization of North Africa and Algeria more specifically), he tries to identify some fundamental common and shared essence in this multiplicity. So what is the essence of colonialism for Fanon?

I want to point out a key insight of Fanon about the essence of colonialism that directly refers to the discussion of the politics of not speaking. I argue that for Fanon, colonialism constitutes a phenomenon of pure and absolute violence that constitutes the end, death, failure, or the termination of reason, thinking, or logos. This is similar to Schmitt: whereas Schmitt refers to war, Fanon thinks of violence, which he understands not as something that is other than reason and thinking, but as the end or collapse of thinking or reasoning. Fanon states that "Colonialism is not a thinking machine, nor a body endowed with reasoning faculties. It is violence in its natural state, and it will only yield when confronted with even greater violence" (60). Thus, colonialism is pure violence that will only yield through violence. Therefore, and this is Fanon's basic point, decolonialization can only happen through violence. This is the core of a text that has inspired a few generations of anticolonial liberation politics based on the premise of armed struggle as the only way to achieve decolonialization. At the core of this is the idea of the end of reason.

I want to look a little more at how and why Fanon says colonialism is pure violence. What does he mean by this, and what is pure violence in this context? Fanon describes what he calls the colonial situation, or the colonial system, as nevertheless a certain system, a certain organizing principle of an entire collective existence. His point is that colonialism is not irrational; likewise, violence is not irrational, anarchic, chaotic. This is similar to Schmitt's argument that war is not simply the lack of reason, but rather contains a very clear logic, in the mode of non-logic, in the mode of rupture of logic. Fanon describes a clear system in his text, sometimes in theological terms.

This is why I think theology is crucial for understanding Fanon, especially via the word *Damnés*, meaning those who are subjected to damnation or curse. It cannot simply be translated as "the wretched" because it does not just refer to people who are poor and miserable, but rather to something in the decolonial situation that is metaphysical, or understood as metaphysical in a theological context. Fanon sometimes uses a theological term, Manichaeism, insofar as he describes the colonial situation as a Manichean situation, a Manichean world. Manichaeism is a Persian religion that became popular at a certain point in the fourth or fifth century in areas that were already Christianized. At a certain moment, it was declared heresy within Christianity. One of the famous Christian philosophers and theologians who wrote against the Manicheans was Augustine. Manichaeism is often understood by Christianity and within later Western intellectual history as rooted in a worldview based on a strong dichotomy between good and evil. Like similar religious movements in late antiquity, sometimes called gnostic, it is based on the idea that we are held prisoners within a fallen, evil world that has been created by an evil god. Yet most of the time, people do not realize the nature of this world and its evil reality. The good lies in a very faraway place, in a very different world—in a good god, a different god—that marks a general direction for hope or redemption in a completely different world, a complete revolution.

Some consider these ideas Christian heresy in the sense that Christianity has one creator god who is also the redeeming god, whereas Manicheanism concerns a split, dual divinity. It believes in a creator who created this evil world and a different, good god. There are different interpretations and versions of this kind of religion. Fanon is not interested in the details of who the Manicheans were but in the dichotomous worldview, a dichotomy within a system—the colonial world—that is basically evil. In this context, the wretched, that is, the colonized, are not just wretched, not just in a poor condition, they are damned (*damnés*). They live in an evil world that they are powerless to change. This connects back to Schmitt's idea of original sin: man is evil not because we act badly, but because when we want to be good, this being is beyond us.

Schmitt's conception of original sin parallels Fanon's idea that the colonized view the colonial world as evil. Colonized people are born into an existence, into an entire system, that is similar to the world created by the bad, evil god. It doesn't matter what they do, how hard they work at school, how moral they want to be, or how much effort and enthusiasm they bring into the world. The world is against them, the colonized, the wretched: they are *damnés*, doomed. Colonialism is an evil god. According to Fanon's analysis of colonialism, it is a sociopolitical situation in which one group has enough

40 | Politics of Not Speaking

power to generate an entire system of ideas, institutions, and economy in which another group is marked cursed and doomed to a life of wretchedness, whereas the first, powerful group is marked good and destined to have a healthy, happy existence. This is why the word "apartheid" has such significance within colonial and decolonial thinking: the idea of separation is crucial. This is why South Africa has become such an important paradigm and why, for example, it is an important term for those critiquing Israeli politics. It refers to the idea of a system of power that is so asymmetrical that it creates a completely different world for different populations.

Fanon describes this extreme—metaphysical in a sense—separation with the terms "species" and "races." At a certain point he says, "This world, divided into compartments, this world cut in two is inhabited by two different species" (39). It is not about different cultures or different religions, but rather two different species. He goes on: "The originality of the colonial context is that economic reality, inequality and the immense difference of ways of life never come to mask the human realities. When you examine at close quarters the colonial context, it is evident that what parcels out the world is to begin with the fact of belonging to or not belonging to a given race, a given species" (40). This is the concrete meaning of being doomed to a certain destiny by birth by the fact of entering a world that is evil for you no matter what. The word "race" refers to this situation; this is what "race" means today as a means of critical analysis in decolonial, postcolonial, and critical race studies. It is important to understand that Fanon does not say that the colonized belong biologically to a different race than the colonizers. He does not offer such a distinction but rather argues that, through the sociopolitical reality that is generated by colonialism, some people are born into a certain group that is doomed. They do not just belong to a different culture, they belong to a different race or species; they were attributed a different kind of humanity at birth. This is important to understand because today, especially in Europe, there is also misunderstanding about what race means in this kind of discourse.

In the place where Fanon was writing, one of the clearest criteria for the distinction between races—but not the only one—is skin color. He speaks more about this in *Black Skins White Masks*. In *The Wretched of the Earth*, the idea of skin color also serves as a means to enact this distinction, one that is not biological but is instead an economic, political, and social distinction between rich, strong populations and poor, weaker ones. It is used to distinguish between the good and bad kinds of humanity: the colonizers and the natives. The word "native" is important: it is a distinction used to designate non-European people who belong to non-European territories that were colonized by Europe. It refers to the concrete reality created by a Manichean world order, the concrete reality of separation. Fanon speaks about how this division (apartheid) is not only geographical but also metaphysical. He argues that the colonial situation creates a certain set of values. In this schema, the damned are understood as doomed because they deserve to be doomed, and they deserve to be doomed because they represent a different and inferior kind of humanity. The natives (colonized) are understood as less than human, as representing some kind of evil. In a world that is evil for them, they are understood to be the principal evil. Fanon goes on:

> The colonial world is a Manichean world. It is not enough for the settler to delimit physically, that is to say with the help of the army and the police force, the place of the native. As if to show the totalitarian character of colonial exploitation, the settler paints the native as a sort of quintessence of evil. Native society is not described simply as a society lacking in values. It is not enough for the colonist to affirm that those values have disappeared from, or still better never existed in, the colonial world. The native is declared insensible to ethics; he represents not only the absence of values, but also the negation of values. He is, let us dare to admit, the enemy of values, and in this sense he is the absolute evil. He is the corrosive element destroying all that comes near him; he is the deforming element, disfiguring all that has to do with beauty or morality; he is the depository of maleficent powers, the unconscious and irretrievable instrument of blind forces. (40)

The colonized, the native, represents evil. The combination of these physical and metaphysical aspects and symbols creates a dehumanizing effect, rendering the natives less than human. As likewise discussed in Heidegger and Schmitt, Fanon describes a shadowy side of European claim to represent universal humanism. The shadow is the assumption that the human is European. This is rooted in the notion that European humanism needs to be brought to other people who do not have humanism, namely those who are in some way less than human. This is what Fanon describes in a concrete, economic, political manner from the perspective of the colonized non-European. It is a critique of this perspective of Europe, of this vision of humanism, that creates violence. It concerns not only a conflict between two sides, but a violence deployed in the name of the good against something

42 | Politics of Not Speaking

understood as evil, less than human. This is Schmitt's analysis, which we now find in Fanon.

We now examine the question of the truth or logos in this context. What is the status of truth or thinking, reason, science, or what Fanon calls objectivity, in this kind of situation? Just how ontologically deep does the state of colonialism go for Fanon? This question is similar to the question of how deep the state of *polemos* or conflict goes for Schmitt, and of how deep the situation of difference goes for Heidegger. Fanon describes a situation in which, for the native, for the *damnés,* or doomed, the world is evil in the sense that any objectivity in the world is already something that works against them. This is understood precisely in the manner in which gnostic or Manichean texts are framed. It is not that people are evil, but that the very physical structure of the world is evil. Our bodies are evil prisons for our souls. Fanon perhaps doesn't go this far (or perhaps he does, as we will see), but he does say that any discourse of truth or objectivity in this situation already works against the native. He argues that:

> The problem of truth ought also to be considered. In every age, among the people, truth is the property of the national cause. No absolute verity, no discourse on the purity of the soul, can shake this position. The native replies to the living lie of the colonial situation by an equal falsehood. His dealings with his fellow-nationals are open; they are strained and incomprehensible with regard to the settlers. Truth is that which hurries on the break-up of the colonialist regime; it is that which promotes the emergence of the nation; it is all that protects the natives, and ruins the foreigners. In the colonialist context there is no truthful behavior: and the good is quite simply that which is evil "for them." (50)

There is a dichotomy, a *polemos*, that works on the level of being, on the level of truth. Truth is not something neutral; rather it is structurally for or against us, because the colonial world is an evil world that is structured to work against the native. Logos breaks here. Logos itself is already broken in the sense that it works against the native. Here we find the description of colonialism as a break of logos, in which the colonial logos itself is the break of speech and discourse. Colonial order, colonial speech, and even dialogue are already violence. This is very similar to Heidegger and the Japanese interlocutor.

What does it mean to be colonized in this context, and to work for decolonization? For Fanon, there is a central tension to the nature of decolonization. His text is not addressing the colonizers (the text is not written for Europeans); it is not a *polemos* with French people, Europeans, or colonizers, and it is not written to persuade Europeans to stop their actions. This would be an impossibility in the colonial cosmos. Rather, the text addresses those who are trying to break from the colonial situation. It is a polemics within the decolonizing movement, *polemos* against other strategies of decolonization. Before we get to Fanon's answer, it is important to examine what he deems problematic. His real adversaries are not colonizers, they are other nonviolent decolonization strategies.

Fanon identifies some agents of decolonization from within the colonized world, such as liberation movements in Algeria and other places at the time. There were many actors looking toward liberation and decolonization within the liberation movement. The central paradigm that he mentions concerns native intellectuals, writers, and academics: people working with logos; experts in discourse, thinking, and thought; people who are steeped in words; people of words. He also sometimes speaks about the commercial elite and political parties. What is common to all these actors is that they are "permeated by colonialism and all its ways of thinking" (44). Fanon asserts that although these actors are native and belong to the race of the damned, they nevertheless attempt to live in a world that is designed in such a way that they cannot win. In different ways, they decide to join the system, work with the colonial way of thinking, and see if they can gain power from within. In sites of intellectual, economic, and political power, they try to integrate, gain some power, and work with the system from within. They try to work with the order, the logic of the situation, the logos. Fanon sometimes refers to this as assimilation, but he also uses the word "emancipation," which is interesting with regard to inner-European processes such as Jewish assimilation. Thus, these natives believe in the possibility of their own or collective emancipation through joining the colonial order, lifting the separation, and becoming one with the colonizers. At a certain moment, Fanon refers to these as "affranchised slaves," or slaves who become friends with the masters and then themselves become masters.

Fanon argues that these strategies are concerned with appeasement rather than overthrowing the established order or breaking the system. It is about achieving peace: stopping the conflict and reaching understanding, harmony, and unity. This is the peace movement. The same terminology is also often used today. For example, Palestinian peace activists in the

44 | Politics of Not Speaking

Israeli-Palestinian conflict are sometimes criticized by militant activists in Fanonian terms for trying to bring about peace in a world that offers them no chance. They cooperate with a system that is structurally oppressing them. They are misguided, or, to use another word that has become important in this context, they believe in dialogue. They believe that one can use the right language, arguments, and reason with the other side to reach an understanding. Fanon lists specific means of decolonization that he understands to be false kinds of decolonization. He asks: "What are the forces that within colonial history open up new outlets and engender new aims for the violence of colonized peoples? In the first place there are political parties and the intellectual or commercial elites. Now, the characteristic feature of certain political structures is that they proclaim abstract principles but refrain from issuing definite commands" (58). They avoid what Schmitt would call the friend-foe decision and instead try to work with words and ideas:

> The entire action of these nationalist political parties during the colonial period is the action of the electoral type. A string of philosophico-political dissertations on the themes of the rights of peoples to self-determination, the rights of man to freedom from hunger and human dignity, and the unceasing affirmation of the principle: One man, one vote. The national political parties never lay stress upon the necessity of a trial of armed strength, for the good reason that their objective is not the radical overthrowing of the system. Pacifists and legalists, they are in fact partisans of order, the new order. On the specific question of violence, the elite are ambiguous. (59)

This passage concerns actors who try to act peacefully within the realm of reason, logos, negotiations, discussions, debates, argumentations, persuasions, and so forth. Fanon refers to them as "philosophico-political dissertations." They remain part of the world and ambiguous about violence, namely about breaking the rules. This politics of nonviolence bothers Fanon. He says that it remains within the order of the world that, as he understands it, is colonial and therefore structurally oppressive toward the natives. This oppression of one group is the raison d'être of colonialism. Any way of trying to be part of this order inescapably leads to further oppression, suppression, and violence.

What is true decolonization? This is the core of the text and Fanon's famous intervention. Once again, theology enters the conversation, this time Christian rather than Manichean. Fanon speaks about the breakdown of the existing world and the creation of a new world, a new humanity, a new language. There must be a demise, a destruction, of the existing order out of which a new order, universe, reality must emerge. He uses the New Testament twice in the text, drawing on Mathew 20:16, "The last shall be the first and the first last" (37, 46). In a corrupt, evil world, the good are doomed and the evil are prosperous. In a just world, the order reverses, and the righteous do well and the evil do not. Fanon speaks about an inverse world in which there are no compromises. Redemption, liberation, and decolonization therefore entail a complete inversion of the world's order. He goes on: "Decolonization never takes place unnoticed, for it influences individuals and modifies them fundamentally. It transforms spectators crushed with their inessentiality into privileged actors, with the grandiose glare of history's floodlights upon them. It brings a natural rhythm into existence, introduced by new men, and with it a new language and a new humanity. Decolonization is the veritable creation of new men" (35). This concerns the creation of a new human being, which is why I describe it as ontological, comparable to Schmitt's theological discussions about the human as well as to Heidegger's understanding of *Dasein*, the human "being-there," or the house of being. In decolonization, there is the need to completely question the colonial being. Fanon underlines that "the last shall be first and the first shall be last." Decolonization entails putting this sentence into practice. It is very similar to Heidegger's eschatology, a similar apocalyptic, messianic vision based on materializing the realm of God and putting it into practice.

Who are the agents of this revolution? Not the intellectuals, not the commercial elites, and not the political parties. These are all agents of the existing order. The agents of the completely new world must be the doomed, the *damnés*, those who come last in the existing world, those who belong to what Fanon calls the peasant masses. Not those in the cities, not those who are located in the hubs of the existing order, who live from the circulation of economic goods, but the peasants. These, he says, have nothing to lose. They will make no compromises. He underlines that, "the *fellah*, the unemployed man, the starving native does not lay a claim to the truth, they do not want to *say* that they represent the truth, for they *are* the truth" (48). They embody reality as it should be. Those of you who are familiar with Marx will recognize the similarity with the proletariat, the class that has lost everything, has nothing to lose, and therefore represents the agents of the revolution. This is very similar to Fanon's argument, and Fanon indeed refers to Marx's analysis. Nonetheless, he claims that the situation of the colonized (the *damnés*) is more radical than that of the proletariat.

46 | Politics of Not Speaking

Q: In this sense, are we closer to Maoism in the sense of the peasantry instead of the proletariat?

A: Exactly. This is what you will find in Mao, the cultural revolution. It doesn't just involve changing the structure of production, as Marx discusses, but a deeper revolution wherein we have to change the way we exist in the world, the entire civilization. This is why it is a non-European kind of Marxism. Fanon invokes these peasant masses as the agents of true decolonialization: those who don't speak the language, those who don't even know how to talk with the French. The nature of decolonization for Fanon is therefore not based on reasoning and is not a rational confrontation. Rather than being about making strong arguments and giving speeches about changing the situation, it is "the untidy affirmation of an original idea propounded as an absolute" (41). It is about land, food, dignity, and people who are not arguing or trying to convince anyone. It is about those who are hungry and want food; those who are dispossessed and need land; and those who are dehumanized and want dignity. In this regard, they are without compromise—there is nothing to argue about. These agents are in absolute, ontic conflict with the colonial world. They are not looking for a way in or for a means to move up. They oppose the entire system and represent the destruction of reality as it is.

It is fascinating how Fanon, who was working in psychiatry within a dispossessed and disempowered colonized population, describes the situation of the decolonial agent on a bodily level: "The native's muscles are always tensed" (53). This comes close to saying that the body itself, its physical nature, is in conflict with the world. The native never feels at home or at ease in the world. There is no relaxation, because the world is an evil, oppressive place, and so the native's muscles are always tensed. The native, the agent of decolonization, exists bodily in the mode of violence, of aggression. It is an aggressive, violent kind of humanity.

This aggression and violence that Fanon describes has two main directions. The first direction—and this is the tragic part of colonization—is the aggression of the native turned against other natives, which he calls auto-destruction. This aggression is turned not outward against the colonizers, but inward within the communities of the colonized. He speaks about different manifestations, such as communities of colonized populations acting out auto-destructive violence within the community, within the home, domestic violence. He speaks of tribal wars, or different communities of natives that attack each other. Fanon also speaks about aggressive fantasies created in this kind of oppressed culture, such as different mythologies that involve monsters, zombies, or terrible creatures that embody this terror of reality projected toward a fantastic world. He speaks about a sublimation of violence into what he understands as libido, a violent sort of erotics that he identifies in forms of orgiastic, ecstatic dance. He interprets these different manifestations within native cultures as manifestations of this basic bodily state of existence in violence, as representing the destruction of and aggression toward the world, an inner, auto-destructive violence.

Fanon is interested in rechanneling this auto-destructive violence into a decolonizing violence, one with the kind of energy that can bring down colonialism. He calls this anti-settler violence, or the violence of the colonized against the colonizers. This is how Fanon understands the good, right, effective violence of decolonization: when the muscles of the oppressed are not addressed toward each other but toward the settlers, the colonizers. This entails natives overcoming the psychological obstacles related to the almost-mythological fear of the settler communities, which is akin to revolting against the gods. This is embedded in the imagination that there is an unlimited amount of colonial power, which makes any resistance hopeless. Fanon tries to show that the colonial powers are not as invincible as the colonized think they are.

One of the important moments of the post-WWII decolonization movement was the defeat of the French in Vietnam. This moment changed the colonial struggle in many ways. For the first time, a colonial power lost and was compelled to leave. Fanon refers to this historical moment, suggesting that the natives need to overcome the mythological power of the settlers and channel their own violence, their muscles, toward the settlers, a moment that he describes as a reversed Manicheism. The same system needs to be reversed and the same mechanics used. He underlines that "On the logical plane, the Manicheism of the settler produces a Manicheism of the native" (92). The creation of race by the colonial system produces a racial worldview of the oppressed. This is present in current dynamics of the discourse on whiteness, blackness, and so forth: a racial discourse that is not racist, but anti-racist. Sartre referred to it as racist anti-racism. So understood, decolonization operates as a Manichean movement, a movement of good against evil. However, it is more accurately a counter-Manichean movement, an anti-racist racism. Fanon writes that the notion of the colonized concerning the absolute evil of the settler responds to the notion of the colonizer concerning the absolute evil of the native. The settlers made the colonized the absolute evil; and to turn it around, the settlers must be made the absolute evil.

48 | Politics of Not Speaking

This discussion involves a kind of decision in the Schmittian sense. The colonized need to decide that the colonizers are their enemies, not their friends. What this implies on the level of action goes back to the question of how this kind of decision is possible. Fanon offers an analysis that points at the need to take an irrevocable action. If one really wants to engage in decolonization, they need to perform an irrevocable action: an action from which they can no longer return, an action that breaks with the order. It is no longer shouting, speaking, saying, arguing, from which one can always return; it is an action that creates a gap, a break, whereby one becomes an enemy of the established order. One becomes hopeless, and, in a sense, they become what they really are: doomed.

Fanon says that at a certain point, there is the need for an action that shows the real nature of the colonized as doomed. This action is the act of violence that outs them as the enemy of the system in an irrevocable way and so, in practice, the colonized becomes an enemy, persecuted, wanted, a criminal. The more violence is committed, the more hopeless the situation becomes, and so the more committed the colonized is to the collapse of the entire system and the better a decolonizer they become. Their only hope at this point is the collapse of the entire order.

There is a theologically infused passage in which Fanon quotes a theater play written by Aimé Césaire, an important decolonial writer who was his teacher in Martinique. It is a dialogue between a rebel and his mother in which the rebel describes how he had been a slave with a master, but then participated in a mutiny and killed the master. He says it was he, the "good slave" (87). Then he faces the master, who is surprised because he was the "good slave, the faithful slave, the slave of slaves, and suddenly his eyes were like two cockroaches, frightened in the rainy season . . . I struck, and the blood spurted." He kills the master, and "that was the only baptism that I can remember today" (88). The blood of the master spilled on him, and he was baptized into redemption from the evil world, the world of sin. At that moment, he became an outlaw; he irreversibly became a criminal without the possibility of redemption in the world as it was. If he were caught, he would be killed. His only hope was to continue the violent struggle to end the world as it was.

At the very end of the text, Fanon describes how, in this situation, violence becomes a positive generative force. He speaks about violence as an action that is all-inclusive and national. He states, "It follows that it is closely involved in the liquidation of regionalism and of tribalism. Thus, the national parties show no pity at all toward the caids and the customary chiefs. Their destruction is preliminary to the unification of the people" (92). On the collective level, there is a violence that also annihilates the structure of the colonized, the native community. It is something that creates a new society of equals. He continues: "At the level of individuals, the violence is a cleansing force. It frees the native from his inferiority complex and from his despair and inaction; it makes him fearless and restores his self-respect. Even if the armed struggle has been symbolic and the nation is demobilized through a rapid movement of decolonization, the people have the time to see that the liberation has been the business of each and all and that the leader has no special merit" (94). The natives thus become part of a community of equals, *fraternité*. "Illuminated by violence, the consciousness of the people rebels against any pacification" (94). The desire to reach peace is the problem. Violence is what is needed.

The point of this was to show you how the analysis of decolonization takes the idea of the break of logos as a principle of a politics that is resistant to a situation that is established by pure violence, namely by a break of logos. Logoclasm against logoclasm.

Q: The idea of truth is interesting here. You mentioned that the peasants represent the truth for Fanon, and we could debate a little about what that means because I fully subscribe to most of your interpretation. But I think that his idea of the peasantry is less glorified. I don't think that's what he aspires to when he's talking about the new man, but rather to a more radical transformation of every position. Is truth something that is already there and comes out, or is the truth in the peasant something that is really going to carry out this radical act of transformation? Is it processual rather than already there? I think it would make a big difference to see it as something that is already there, given, something to emulate, rather than the idea of the truth in the peasant because he is willing to take this step toward the transformation, not only of the system, but also of himself. He also talks about a concept of humanity in which violence is liberating for the colonized, and ultimately also for the colonizer.

A: It goes back to the creation of a new humanity: at the end of days, this dichotomy between good and evil will no longer exist. There is a vision of fraternity beyond these divisions, there is indeed a radical transformation, a new man. But Fanon does not only speak about the native culture in Africa in terms of oppression and as doomed, tense, and aggressive. He also quickly references an original culture of nonviolence, an African

50 | Politics of Not Speaking

culture of resolving conflicts in a nonviolent way. He speaks about village assemblies and local communities where people negotiate their grievances and problems. Regardless of whether it's true, it contains a kind of vision of a world without violence, a noncolonial world. It not only reverses the order of violence, it goes beyond violence toward a new humanity, which nonetheless arises from native cultures. Their existence is not limited to colonization. Fanon hints at the *négritude* movement in this text, suggesting that this could be inspired by non-European or African cultures. He says that it is an African invention. In the moment that he points in this direction, there is a kind of eschatology that goes beyond the Manichean world of good and evil.

Q: I am interested in the links between Fanon's thought, Schmitt's existential struggle, and Heidegger's aim to find a way to something that he calls the other beginning. How does Fanon think about this moment of what the days after look like? How does he deal with the heritage of colonialism? Is violence something that burns everything?

A: There is a similar problem with Heidegger and the kinds of eschatologies that take seriously the fact that they are before eschatology, that in the state of before eschatology one cannot pretend to already know the end. Thus, in the sense of before, one needs to play the game of the non-redeemed, evil, or Manichean world. One needs to be violent, to take sides. One should not be tempted to pretend that redemption has already taken place, to be reasonable and make compromises. At the same time, these thinkers or intellectual movements nonetheless do want to go beyond violence. There is some kind of a promise that is always being made more or less explicitly in Fanon and Heidegger. My critique in this context is that Heidegger goes too deep in this moment of linguistic redemption when we sing together from the same source. In Fanon, this is not the case; it ends with violence. Yet throughout the text there are some hints; the African invention of nonviolent politics is this kind of a moment of promise. He doesn't indulge in *négritude*, but he has this kind of vision of a new humanity after violence.

Q: It's similar in his psychiatric practice too. He's committed to a rationalist psychiatric methodology in many respects; he's using all the latest techniques and equipment; he's performing sleep and shock therapy. At the same time, he looks at the Algerian treatment of mad people and sees what they have that is less moralizing, more human, in their treatment of mad people. He is really trying to combine thought systems and find points of transformation in both. Obviously, that is not worked out in great detail, but combining these things is a point of interest. I think that his reference to the African communities is interesting, akin to what he says about the peasants as well, that their kind of conviviality could be useful for the struggle. The intellectuals are within the colonial framework and are privileged vis à vis the peasants, and this is why the peasants are more revolutionary. The intellectuals should put themselves in the service of the peasants or come together with them. If they pretend that they are proletarians and lead the struggle, the peasants will just scorn them. Thus, there is also this discourse about how to bring people together. This is the fundamental question: how do we come together?

A: Fanon brings to light something that is important for him as an intellectual, precisely this native kind of intellectual that he is writing against, someone who is educated and works in France and speaks the language of the colonizers. It is a moment in which truth is connected to logos. One can reasonably discuss and debate the nature of reality, but this also implies that one could hypothetically reach an objective perception of a reality that could unite people. The reality he describes is one in which truth is already partial in that the differences are so fundamental that there is no sense in talking about something that the colonizers and colonized can agree upon, around which they can reach some kind of agreement. It goes so deep that the only truth that can unite them is the fact that they are in conflict with each other. The peasantry represents this truth. Why? They have nothing, and in order to exist, they need to struggle. They are the truth. Nevertheless, I think that in these moments when he speaks about a new humanity, a new language, a new man, he has a vision in which there will be a different kind of being and therefore a different kind of truth.

Of course, one should also question the status of this kind of logos that he produces. Sartre reads this in Paris and writes that he understands and subscribes to this idea. What is the status of this? Can it even happen? There are the same contradictions found in the communist idea of the proletariat. There are the communists who know: Marx knows, Marx wrote a manifesto. Then there are the workers in the factory: in a sense they don't know, but the whole point is that they don't know. They represent their interests and are the driving force that he is not. There is a tension there: the communists are the bourgeois with access to education and somehow

52 | Politics of Not Speaking

did understand, so they became militant and so forth. It's the same complex situation, I think, of Fanon vis à vis the peasantry. It's the story of two different agents who nonetheless fulfil some truth, agents of different messianic moments.

Corollary I

On the Boycott, Divestment, Sanctions (BDS) Movement

I wish to offer a reflection on modes of active intervention in the so-called Israel-Palestine conflict. These modes include refusing to engage in conversation, rejecting dialogue, and avoiding discussion or debate, namely not speaking. The kind of "not speaking" I am speaking about is not just a lack of action, but a refrainment from action; it is something like active inaction, an active gesture of not speaking, an active gesture of refusing or breaking off communication. I am thinking about not speaking within a communicative space, within a space of speaking, within an already ongoing conversation such that the "not" speaking is in fact an active interruption. Such active, interruptive not speaking, which is paradigmatic and personally concerns me, and us, is the refusal of communication or cooperation within academia, which is an institution of speaking.

What I now wish to reflect upon with you more concretely is the refrainment by Palestinian academics from cooperating with Israeli academics or academic institutions as an intervention in the so-called Israel-Palestinian conflict. There are various forms this active communicative inaction takes, the most well-known, coordinated, and articulate being the academic boycott declared and carried out within the BDS movement.

When I speak here about the BDS movement, I am referring to some basic texts, such as the "Call for Academic and Cultural Boycott of Israel" of 2004, the "Palestinian Civil Society Call for Boycott, Divestment and Sanctions Against Israel until it Complies with International Law and Universal Principles of Human Rights" of July 9, 2005, also known as the "BDS Call," the "Palestinian Campaign for the Academic and Cultural Boycott of Israel (PACBI) Guidelines for the International Academic Boycott

54 | Politics of Not Speaking

of Israel of August 2010," and a series of texts by one of the movement's leaders, Omar Barghouti.[1]

The situation in which the BDS movement seeks to intervene, the so-called Israeli-Palestinian conflict, is conceptualized by these BDS texts in explicitly anticolonial terms, which conform with Fanonian discourse. The political reality of the Israeli-Palestinian constellation is characterized as a situation of structural oppression of the Palestinians by the Israeli order. This system of oppression or apartheid manifests itself in three basic ways: military occupation of Palestinians in the territories occupied in 1967, racial discrimination against Palestinians who are citizens of Israel, and nonrecognition of Palestinian refugees of 1948. Similarly to Fanon's colonial situation, the Israeli situation, according to the BDS texts, is founded on an oppressive logos, which excludes the existence of the Palestinian subject. We may say that the emergence of Palestinian political subjectivity, i.e., the unified figure of the Palestinian in Israel, in the occupied territories, and in the diaspora beyond this split signifies the break with the Israeli logos.

Furthermore, some texts suggest that the structurally oppressive logos is not only Israeli, but international. They point to complicity between Israel and the powers that be, mainly the United States and the UN, in what Omar Barghouti, concerning the Israeli siege of Gaza, calls an "international conspiracy of complicity and silence" (180). This description evokes the notion that Palestinian liberation from oppression must refuse not only the Israeli discourse, but the entire existing international order, all ruling logos.

Similarly to Fanon, and to a greater extent, the logoclastic gesture of the BDS movement, especially as articulated in Omar Barghouti's texts, emphasizes the danger that Palestinian resistance runs in any attempt to enter into dialogue with the existing Israeli discourse. Since this order of discourse is structurally oppressive to the Palestinian subject, any dialogue that takes place within the Israeli discourse in an attempt to bring "change though persuasion" (102) will necessarily generate oppression. In other words, any dialogue with the Israeli system by definition implies violence done to the Palestinian subject. The violence done by dialogue is the most dangerous kind of violence, since it is not experienced as violence, or even conflict. It is experienced as the exact opposite, as peace. In fact, peace, or "normalization," is perceived as the greatest danger, as the greatest enemy, of logoclasm. Within the existing discourse, any normalization is an attempt to "normalize the abnormal" such that any peace is necessarily "devoid of justice" and accordingly constitutes a "sham peace," an illusion.

The BDS movement has, in fact, emerged in the aftermath of the collapse of the attempted peace process of the Oslo Accords. The failed understandings established in the Oslo process are a central target of the BDS critique of the dangerous illusion of the Israel-dominated discourse. What Barghouti's texts criticize most fundamentally is not even the peace, but the perception of the relationship between Israelis and Palestinians not as a system of asymmetrical oppression, but as an alleged "conflict," as a so-called Israeli-Palestinian conflict with supposedly two equal parties. According to Barghouti's critique, within this illusion of conflict, Oslo generated the illusion of an Israeli peace-loving partner, the Zionist left; and the illusion of a so-called Palestinian Authority, whose establishment normalized and institutionalized the ongoing oppression. Oslo has become the symbol for the inherent violence toward Palestinians in any dialogue with Israel and so for the necessity of a new Palestinian politics of not speaking.

Inasmuch as the BDS discourse applies the Fanonian analysis of structurally oppressive colonial logos to the Israeli-Palestinian situation, it also rejects the paradigmatic anticolonial logoclastic politics of armed resistance, of not speaking in the form of violence. This is a major paradigm shift in the history of the Palestinian struggle, and Barghouti's texts defend the nonviolent nature of fighting Israel's domination by means of boycott vis-à-vis the tradition of armed struggle, which—following Fanon—considered any nonviolence as "appeasement," namely as making peace with oppression.

In contrast to the politics of not speaking by way of violence, by way of completely rejecting the order of discourse, the logoclastic operation of the BDS movement is carried out in the realm of discourse: the boycott is a speech act. This can be seen in the fact that the primary and paradigmatic target and site for the BDS movement's boycott is academic, cultural, and intellectual institutions. One common and misguided critique of the BDS movement is that it picked the wrong target in Israeli intellectuals and academics, who are more open to dialogue with the Palestinians and therefore the last who should be boycotted. This critique misunderstands the basic nature of the BDS movement as a negative speech act, which intervenes logoclastically, as rupture and interruption of discourse, precisely at the heart of the institutions that generate discourse, such as universities.[2] BDS is resistance to discourse within discourse.

This observation leads me to questions that concern the gap between the BDS movement's Fanonian analysis of the situation in anticolonial terms and the decidedly non-Fanonian nature of the BDS politics, which does

56 | Politics of Not Speaking

not consist in nondiscursive violence but in speech acts. I wonder under what conditions and in what way, namely with what consequences, within a Fanonian situation, namely a situation of an absolutely corrupt and oppressive order of discourse, effective resistance to this order could nonetheless be discursive. I see two answers, which correspond to two aspects of the BDS movement's academic boycott. Both answers suggest that, to be effective, nonviolent boycott requires that the order of discourse not be entirely corrupt and that the situation not be entirely Fanonian and, in this sense, perhaps not entirely colonial in Fanon's sense, that is, not entirely Manichean.

One aspect of the boycott is the refusal of Palestinian academics to institutionally cooperate—"speak"—with Israeli academics. If one of the central functions of the Israeli logos as colonial is to generate the semblance of peace, of normality, then the failure to do so, shown by the coordinated disengagement by Palestinian academics, may generate a disruption of the Israel-dominated discourse and at least prevent the effacement of oppression by rendering visible the Palestinian subject as excluded from the existing conversation. This might be a nonviolent resistance strategy that Fanon underestimated. However, the effectiveness of such nonengagement, its actual disturbing effect on the Israeli discourse, depends on a critical number of Palestinian academics already being engaged—and therefore missed—in the Israeli conversation, which would mean that the discourse underlying this conversation is not entirely corrupt.

The second aspect of the academic boycott is much more central: it consists not in Palestinian academics refusing to speak with Israeli academics, but in Palestinian academics calling upon international academia to boycott Israeli institutions. Herein lies the power of the BDS movement. This BDS "call" is, however, a positive speech act: it engages in the ongoing international academic conversation in an attempt to persuade, to convince, to change people's minds. In other words, the international BDS call does not condemn the dominant order of discourse like Fanon did. On the contrary, the BDS call consistently refers to and bases itself on a very clear discursive and normative foundation, namely international law and UN resolutions. Notwithstanding Barghouti's remarks on "international conspiracy of complicity and silence," the immediate trigger for the initial "Call for Academic and Cultural Boycott of Israel" of 2004 was the Advisory Opinion of the International Court of Justice (ICJ) from the same year, which declared Israeli colonization illegal. The boycott is demanded as a "sanction" for this law violation. The call to boycott Israel even refers to an already existing precedent, the boycott of South Africa.

In contrast to Fanon's *damnés*, who are structurally condemned by the existing global order, the Palestinian BDS movement therefore acknowledges the basic legitimacy of international law, which would arguably function as a common logos, a shared discursive space for a possible conversation between Palestinians and the Israeli State. If such a discursive space does exist, what could the justification for a politics of not speaking be?

A possible answer would draw on Carl Schmitt, pointing out that the law, especially international law, is not logos; on the contrary, it is the mode of speech that performs the basic human condition of logoclasm, namely of the impossibility of collective existence through pure reasoning and the necessity of war and sovereign decisions. The Palestinian refusal to dialogue would signify—in the face of refused recognition by Israel of Palestinian political sovereignty—the performance of a sovereign act, namely a declaration of independence, an act of political self-constitution, by way of not speaking.

4

Can't Speak: Gayatri Chakravorty Spivak

Our discussion first dealt with Schmitt and the politics of logoclasm as war, and it then moved to Heidegger and looked more concretely at essential difference. Whereas Schmitt's politics don't really get into the question of difference itself—different cultures, systems of discourse, or kinds of logos—Heidegger looks at logos between different cultures: the encounters, mis-encounters, or dis-encounters between cultures and where language or conversation becomes problematic and even takes on the form of danger and violence. This concerns language itself as a form of violence, which we already saw in Schmitt with his criticism of the political ethos of eternal discussion that can turn into politics of war on war.

In Heidegger, the same danger arises with the ideology or ethos of conversation. He speaks less about war than does Schmitt. He instead speaks about a different kind of violence, a certain overtaking, occupation, conquest, or colonialism—a word ("colonialism") that he does not use but that I am inserting into this conversation—of a certain form of culture, civilization, logos of the other. He writes about the relationship between Europe and East Asia as a paradigmatic encounter between thinkers, philosophers, intellectuals, and languages. However, as we already saw, there are political consequences to this asymmetrical encounter. Even the word "encounter" is misleading because this exchange between European civilization and non-European worlds can be more of an occupation than an encounter. In Heidegger we already saw how dialogue can be a form of colonization and the dangers it harbors. Unlike Schmitt, who presents war as the only possible reality of logoclasm, Heidegger tries to offer some sort

60 | Politics of Not Speaking

of conversation, or *Gespräch*, that is not metaphysical, not with signs. What is exchanged is gestures: *Winke*.

Yesterday we moved to a more recent formulation of the same set of issues, politically speaking, but more explicitly in the context of colonialism. The question, the theme, the discourse of decolonialization is based on something that can be understood as the relationship between politics and logos. I presented Frantz Fanon as a thinker who lays down basic ideas of decolonial, anticolonial, and postcolonial discourse, and I argued that these different ideas can be brought together as oriented around the idea of a world based on the collapse of logos, what Fanon calls pure violence. This is how he characterizes the colonial situation.

A common thread in my discussion of all three thinkers is that the break of logos is not simply the absence of logos. It does not entail a chaotic world; it is actually a very organized system, and an extreme mode of failure or end of logos, a certain logoclasm, organizes this very orderly system based on a break or split of humanity. This is how Fanon describes it, as a Manichean colonizer system of settlers and natives. Consequently, for Fanon, the only way out of this situation is to turn this mis-logic around, to recreate a Manichean form of action in which the values are reversed. The settlers become evil, the natives or colonized represent the truth, and the only course of action is pure violence that breaks the order, breaks the broken logos. He problematizes attempts to engage in dialogue or negotiations with the existing order as part of the system of violence.

Today's discussion jumps two and a half decades forward to the late eighties, to one of the most well-known postcolonial philosophers or theorists, an Indian scholar who teaches in the United States, Gayatri Chakravorty Spivak. We will focus on one of Spivak's most influential texts, "Can the Subaltern Speak?" (1988).[1] Thirty-five years later, it is one of the canonic texts of postcolonial theory. With respect to Fanon, it is written from within a different generation of decolonial thought. It is already a critical reflection within decolonial discourse itself about its own problems and challenges. It therefore represents the logical or conceptual next stage, perhaps even two stages, beyond Fanon in trying to understand the colonial situation. It tries to understand the dangers, problems, and challenges and possible ways of dealing with this changing situation as a political and intellectual endeavor.

The title hints at the main issue in the text: the postcolonial question in terms of language. The question is whether the subaltern can speak, so a question regarding speech. Spivak is well-known for her difficult way of

Can't Speak: Gayatri Chakravorty Spivak | 61

writing, and, like Heidegger and Derrida, this is not a coincidence. If one recognizes politics as a question of language in this fundamental way, then one's own acts of language, speech acts, have a political value. If one is talking about difference, then one will try to perform difference, interruption, or a break of language in their own language. Writing in a difficult way is not just an editorial comment; it is already the issue, already a question. What does it mean to speak or write in a difficult way? Whether it is not readable or whether it is readable are central questions, not only epistemologically, but also politically. Spivak writes difficult texts, and there are certain demands and efforts involved in trying to understand what she is saying. There are many things that she takes from Derrida, not least this performance of language, and tomorrow we will speak about Derrida and see how important performance in, of, or from language is for him. Spivak is influenced by Derrida, and this is very clear in this text. He is one of the authors she engages with. He is the author or name that she brings in at the conceptual conclusion of the text. For Spivak, Derrida is a sort of horizon that opens up certain ways of dealing with the difficulties she is addressing.

One expression that Spivak uses in this text to capture the central problem or issue at work in this text and that is intimately connected to our seminar is "epistemic violence." We will start by reading a passage in which she talks about epistemic violence, which provides a beginning. Spivak states that:

The clearest available example of such epistemic violence is the remotely orchestrated, far-flung, and heterogeneous project to constitute the colonial subject as Other. This project is also the asymmetrical obliteration of the trace of that Other in its precarious Subjectivity. It is well known that Foucault locates epistemic violence, a complete overhaul of the episteme, in the redefinition of sanity at the end of the European eighteenth century. What if that particular redefinition was only a part of the narrative of history in Europe as well as in the colonies? What if the two projects of epistemic overhaul worked as dislocated and unacknowledged parts of a vast two-handed engine? Perhaps it is no more than to ask that the subtext of the palimpsestic narrative of imperialism be recognized as "subjugated knowledge," a whole set of knowledges that have been disqualified as inadequate to their task or insufficiently elaborated: naïve knowledges, located low

62 | Politics of Not Speaking

> down on the hierarchy, beneath the required level of cognition
> or scientificity. (280-81)

In this passage, Spivak quotes Foucault's *Power/Knowledge*. Foucault will soon become an enemy, but for now he is an ally. The problem revolves around knowledge. Episteme, as in epistemic violence, means something like science in Greek. It does not just mean knowledge, it is knowledge that is already reflexive, methodical. Today it is often translated as science, but it is not necessarily science. It is rather an authoritative discourse of knowledge in society; it is not just knowledge in the sense of what people say and know, it is what is acknowledged within a certain culture as true, real. We could also use the word truth, but Foucault calls it "episteme." We are talking about epistemic violence. For our purposes, we could just as well call it logical violence, or violence of logos related to what I called speaking, talking, or dialogue as belonging to the realm of politics or the organized kind of social happening.

The question of knowledge and language is very present in Spivak's text. The central issue here is epistemic violence and colonialism. This entails understanding colonialism as enacting not just physical violence, such as Schmitt's ideas of physical violence as killing, but also, as we already saw in Heidegger, violence in speech and language. This likewise connects to Fanon's discussion of the danger in native actors trying to be part of a world that is structurally built against them and the problematic attempt to decolonize through dialogue. For him, violence is created when these efforts mask and become complicit in the violence of the world of the colonizers. Spivak joins these voices to say that there is violence inherent in the act of the production of knowledge in language. She speaks more specifically about the colonial situation. Epistemic violence in this context is connected to the "project to constitute the colonial subject as Other" (280–81). This is the core of what she is talking about, namely that epistemic violence, violence of knowledge or logos, is somehow connected to a constitution of the colonial subject. There is a colonial subject, what Fanon called "the colonized," that is being constituted through colonial knowledge, through the logos of the discourse of imperialist powers.

Foucault locates epistemic violence in what Spivak says is a complete overhaul of the episteme, namely where one culture, subculture, world, or system of understanding, speaking, and knowing takes over and silences another. This is a dynamic of difference, a violent dynamic in which the encounter between different worlds creates an event of violence from one

Can't Speak: Gayatri Chakravorty Spivak | 63

world on another, a complete overhaul of epistemes. It results in the obliteration of one culture. Spivak quotes the idea of "subjugated knowledge," the idea that cultures of knowledge can be subjugated. People can not only be physically subjugated, but their entire set of knowledges can be subjugated and disqualified as insufficient. There are different mechanisms through which different cultures of knowledge can be subjugated, "naïve knowledges, located low down on the hierarchy, beneath the required level of cognition or scientificity" (281). As discussed earlier, decolonial thinkers sought to show that humanism has a dark side in which non-European cultures are understood as not being humanist or human enough. The dehumanization, the hierarchization of cultures of knowledge, leads to a politics of subjugation, an overhaul of non-European cultures of knowledge. This is what Fanon discusses, and Spivak discusses this via Foucault in "Can the Subaltern Speak?"

Spivak also critiques Foucault, which is something I want to underline from the beginning. As I have said, Foucault is a friend for now but will soon become an enemy. Foucault, Spivak says, locates epistemic violence, a complete overhaul of the episteme, in the redefinition of sanity at the end of the European eighteenth century. For Foucault, it is about events, processes of epistemic violence within the development of modern Europe. The question of sanity is not important now. Foucault has different moments, one of them being the history of sanity and insanity. The important thing is that he locates these kinds of epistemic violence in the processes of the development of modern culture in Europe that take over other European cultures, subjects, forms of knowledge, and epistemes. With respect to this kind of epistemic violence, Spivak asks:

> [is it] only a part of the narrative of the history in Europe as well as in the colonies? What if this event that Foucault identifies as epistemic violence that is constitutive to our present time, to the European modern time, was not only taking part within Europe? What if the two projects of epistemic overhaul worked as dislocated and unacknowledged parts of the vast two-handed engine. Perhaps it is no more than to ask that the subtext of the palimpsestic narrative of imperialism be recognized as "subjugated knowledge." (281)

Imperialism and colonialism should be understood not only in terms of physical violence and economic exploitation, but also as an epistemic kind

64 | Politics of Not Speaking

of violence, which brings us back to our theme of logos as violence. There are various people working from postcolonial perspectives who have thematized epistemic violence. A few years ago, there was an important book by Boaventura de Sousa Santos about epistemicide, a concept that speaks not only about genocide, or the killing of peoples, but also about colonial history that includes the killing or destruction of cultures of knowledge. This idea is mainly discussed in the context of the Global South. In Spivak's text, there is the idea of subjugated knowledge, or a culture of knowledge, a language that is silenced through a violent encounter or conversation. The idea of constituting the other of Europe is central here. There is a specific violence that Spivak focuses on in this epistemic assault, particularly how discourse, knowledge, ideas, and conversation constitute the other. European knowledge constitutes the other of Europe, namely the colonized, the non-European, the native.

In the idea of language that creates silence, there is also the idea of giving voice to the other. Upon a cursory glance, it is the opposite of silencing. It almost works in complete contrast to the described processes of subjugation or repression: silencing, obliterating, destroying, and annihilating. In this context, language is constituting: giving image, words, a face, and a voice to the other. It is creating the other, but this is precisely the main act of violence that Spivak discusses. The violence is not the erasure of the other, it is the constitution of the other. This is the important act of violence because it doesn't look like an act of violence but rather like an emancipatory act. Think of how Count Kuki tried to give voice to Japanese art in the language of European metaphysics, which Heidegger saw as a type of death. He was trying to give language, to express, to understand; and that was a gift of death. There is a similar issue in Spivak's text, spoken now in the language of the other of Europe.

Spivak talks about the colonial project in terms of its entry into the civilizations of others, or how European knowledge penetrates and invades cultures of non-European civilizations and takes over their languages from within. She mentions two concrete ways in which this kind of taking over was enacted through historiography and legislation, namely the acts of giving language to the others to write their histories, create their narratives, and to express their norms of life via legislation. On the one hand, this can be enacted completely from the outside, as in the example of the British entering India and creating a system of administration, courts, police, and so forth that literally created the laws and wrote the history of India. This becomes a more subtle, dangerous violence—to use Fanon's words—when the natives take over and learn how to write their own history in the language of the British. They do so not just in English words, but also through adopting this language as a whole way of thinking. In this example, Indians learn how to make their own laws through the ideas and language of the British administration. The colonial power is not only telling, teaching the other to tell, narrate, and portray themselves in the language of Europe, it is also giving them the tools to concretely shape their political and social life via norms and legislation.

Spivak points to a specific location within the colonial administration of epistemic violence, where she identifies a problem in what she calls the margins, more specifically the subaltern classes. "Subaltern" is a concept that was coined by Gramsci, an important Italian Marxist thinker who was already thinking beyond Marx or developing some aspects in Marxist thought in the realm of culture and knowledge. He spoke about "hegemony," one of his important concepts, and in a sense was already examining many of the things that we are talking about here, such as epistemic violence, or violence within discourse. Gramsci designates the subaltern as those who are weak or wretched, those who are subjugated by the stronger culture.

Spivak's subaltern are not the proletariat, who are already a part of the system. Akin to Fanon's discussion of the peasant, here is a kind of subjugation that is more radical than that of the proletariat, the people who are not even inside of or part of the system, who are more radically repressed. This is the subaltern. Spivak wants to thematize the question of epistemic violence through the question of the subaltern. In a way, the subaltern is analogous to what Fanon was talking about with the peasant, the part of the native population that is not even part of the system. They do not study at the universities; they do not get to climb the echelons of politics or economy. They are outside of these spheres; they don't have a place in the order. Beyond Marx's proletariat, they are those who are the truth of the situation, namely those who experience the violence of the colonial situation in their bodies and existence.

In her text, Spivak asks if the subaltern can speak. Can these people who embody the truth of the colonial situation, namely those who have no place in this world, nonetheless speak? Do they have a place in the discourse? Spivak claims that the most problematic form of epistemic violence is paradoxically perpetrated by creating the illusion that the subaltern can speak, creating the impression, the notion, that those who are structurally subjugated by the order of discourse, by order, by knowledge, are nonetheless part of and have some agency in a system based on their exclusion. This is the problematic form of epistemic violence that Spivak thematizes. In more general terms, she speaks about the notion of the sovereign subject, again as a certain figure of epistemic violence, a discourse, knowledge, form of culture that creates an illusion or idea of a sovereign subject.

In this context, the connection between logos and subject is important to understand. The sovereign subject—think of Schmitt's sovereign state—is a subject that is in absolute possession of itself. It knows itself, controls itself, is connected to some kind of dream of the emancipation or enlightenment of human reason. It is a completely autonomous subject of modern knowledge, of European humanism, that Spivak, following others such as Derrida and Heidegger, criticizes as problematic. It is a notion that is conveyed in, through, and as European knowledge and that holds a very deep form of violence by creating the illusion that the subaltern can speak, is a sovereign subject, is in complete possession of a wholesome, functioning, continuous logos or reasoning.

The problem of the sovereign subject is not only the illusion of the subaltern. The European discourse itself, its own knowledge of itself, creates the idea of the European sovereign subject, the European human being that is imported to or propagated toward the outside. This figure itself is a problem. This is analogous to the idea of the state of law as a state of logos in Schmitt. The sovereign state as a state of complete rational order is analogous to the state of the subject as a sovereign subject, a certain figment, fiction—not only in the sense of a complete lie, but in the sense of a production—that Spivak criticizes. I want to explore how this is connected to the idea of logos. Spivak criticizes this idea in the colonial context as leading to a problematic type of politics, namely imperial colonial politics. I want to look at the two places in which Spivak locates this problematic kind of politics and production of the appearance of a sovereign subject in the colonial context.

The two historical scenes in Spivak's text locate imperial epistemic violence in the form of the constitution, or the invention, of the speaking subaltern. The first scene is the colonial organization, mechanism of power itself. She speaks about this at the end of the text. Spivak looks at the British administration in colonial India. She speaks about the British abolition of widow sacrifice, what is called the *sati*; and there are already a lot of problems in the word and the language used to describe it. According to the already well-established historiographical narrative at the time of this text, certain Indian cultures have a ritual in which the death of an important person results in their widow's sacrifice. This happens while the body of the deceased is being burned; the still-alive widow is burned with the body of the dead husband as an act of sacrifice or self-sacrifice. There was a moment, early in the British colonial administration of India, when the British authorities decided to abolish this ritual, to legally prohibit any performance of it. Spivak focuses on the figure of the burned woman to speak about the woman subaltern. She stresses that within marginalized groups, there are those who are marginalized in the margins. Thus, there is the subaltern and the women subaltern, who faces another layer of repression. Spivak argues that in this situation, namely the abolition of this ritual, one can see colonial epistemic violence at work in the fiction of the subaltern who can speak.

How does this come about? One can already see that this shows the ambivalences of colonialism. For the colonizers, it seems like a good thing to abolish this ritual, to save these women from repression and death. It seems like precisely the kind of act that could support the idea that colonialism and imperialism were not all bad, that they brought progress and emancipation and liberation to some parts of the population. It is precisely in this instance of what seems to be a positive moment brought through colonization, a moment of logos, of giving voice, that Spivak points out a problem.

Where does she locate the problem? Spivak sketches a situation in which there is a dialectic: there are two discourses that are being produced through this colonial abolition of the *sati* sacrifice. There is the imperial discourse, the discourse of the British authorities who wish to prohibit, abolish, and stop this act from taking place. Spivak offers a formulation that problematizes the situation: she calls it white men saving brown women from brown men. In this context, the British colonizer saves the colonized women from the colonized men. The subaltern woman becomes an instrument through which white men oppress brown men. Spivak more specifically points at how colonial power constructs the figure of the human in the discussion and conversation around this ritual, its prohibition, and the figure of the Indian woman and widow. It involves the subject as a certain figure of European understanding of the individual that the British feel is violated in this ritual.

Spivak shows how, according to British discourse, the free will of these women is being violated; namely, they have a certain sovereignty, a certain self-understanding of themselves, a certain will that is being violated by this act. Spivak argues that this European discourse plants an understanding of the human being in the subaltern situation of these rituals. Again, regardless

68 | Politics of Not Speaking

of the question of whether this is good or bad, Spivak shows how a ritual is decontextualized from its cultural context and becomes an act of aggression against a European understanding of what it means to be human or a subject, namely this idea of free will. She provocatively suggests that one could have also interpreted this ritual in the same way that Europeans understand, for example, military conscription in which people are taken against their will to serve a higher cause, like the protection of the state or, in earlier times, to serve God. Spivak says that there is a way of interpreting this ritual that was decontextualized and simply understood as murder. In doing so, a construction was made of the Indian woman as a sovereign subject whose desires and wishes were being violated through his ritual.

Spivak demonstrates how through the colonial construction of the sacrificed women as sovereign, willing subjects who can speak, a counter construction was generated by traditionalist opposition to British policies on these rituals. She says that this colonial act created a counter-act by traditional native proponents of this ritual and of native culture that once again produces, paradoxically, the figure of the woman subaltern as a sovereign subject. The native counterargument to white men saving brown women from brown men is that these women want to die. They have free will and their will is to die, because this is their way of showing their commitment to their husbands and their families, their will to be good wives. Spivak says this is a counternarrative in which the value of the women's will is being inverted while the fiction of the sovereign subject is being maintained and even reinforced. The same fiction of the subaltern woman as nonetheless possessing will, logos, power is reproduced, now by the natives against colonialism.

Spivak argues that these two conflicting voices in the colonial situation, the colonial authority and the natives, create two fictions of a speaking woman subaltern. These two fictions of a speaking woman ultimately efface women. This is the way that the subaltern is produced, through the fiction of the self as a sovereign subject in which these two forms of conflicting discourses, the two logoi, are imposed. In this production of the subaltern, epistemic violence is enacted through the creation of the speaking subaltern in the historical colonial situation. Spivak ends her text with this idea.

She begins her text with a second historical moment, which is no longer the colonial scene, but rather a postcolonial moment. This is the real thrust of the text. As I have already said, it is already a critical reflection within postcolonial discourse itself, within the critique of colonialism. Spivak points to how the same epistemic violence by constituting the figure of the speaking subaltern is reproduced within postcolonial discourse. Where does she see this? The text begins with Spivak not looking back on colonial history but on Western French intellectual discourse. This is a discourse that takes place in a country that historically occupied the role of colonizer, but it is nevertheless a discourse that is already critical in the terms of the postcolonial age. Beyond this, the specific intellectual, one of the two she quotes, is one who is originally an ally in this text, Foucault. Spivak uses the example of Foucault and Gilles Deleuze, not to criticize them specifically, but rather to criticize a certain gesture or way of talking and Western critique of the West: a critique of the West by the West, a critique of the subject, a critique of the very notion of the subject that she herself problematizes. To do so, Spivak discusses intellectuals who agree with her on some basic level.

As already discussed, Foucault understands epistemic violence: he developed the entire theory of epistemic violence and showed how it historically unfolds. Spivak now takes Foucault and Deleuze as examples of two Western intellectuals who are critical of the West and the subject and illustrates how their discourse reproduces the epistemic violence that she pointed out in the colonial situation, namely epistemic violence through the constitution of the appearance of the subaltern that can nonetheless speak. This is done once again through an act of seeming empowerment. This is where violence is concealed. The act that we are talking about now is not the abolition of the burning ritual, but something that seems more benign, more prosaic, more intellectual, scholarly. It is a speech act in a conversation between intellectuals in which the Western intellectual is aware of the problem of epistemic violence and distances himself from the colonized culture. He declares silence; he performs logoclasm by saying that he cannot speak for the subaltern, cannot represent the oppressed. This involves a critical action of distancing, of self-silencing, to give space to the voice of the other. Spivak gives the example of how Foucault speaks about the masses who know or how Deleuze speaks about prisoners who can speak for themselves: "Foucault articulates another corollary of the disavowal of the role of ideology in reproducing the social relations of production: an unquestioned valorization of the oppressed as subject, the 'object being,' as Deleuze admiringly remarks, 'to establish conditions where the prisoners themselves would be able to speak.' Foucault adds that 'the masses *know* perfectly well, clearly'—once again the thematic of being undeceived 'they know far better than [the intellectual] and they certainly say it very well' " (274). Spivak quotes two moments of discussion between Deleuze

70 | Politics of Not Speaking

and Foucault that illustrate how, in an attempt to give space, these two intellectuals create a fiction of the oppressed speaking for themselves. She criticizes another group of intellectuals whose texts perform a similar act, an Indian group of scholars—think of Fanon's native intellectual—called the Subaltern Studies Group. This is a group of mostly historians and sociologists that was established in India and is still important and working today. They are trying to create a postcolonial kind of historiography of India in which history will not be told from the perspective of the colonizer but from the perspective of the people, of the peasants. Spivak's argument is complex, and I do not go into it here, but she shows how this group was aware that there was a problem of understanding these peasants, this subaltern group, as a sovereign subject. It is a problem of understanding identity in difference, and also of understanding this group as completely conscious of itself. Nonetheless, she argues that once again and ultimately, the Subaltern Studies Group creates the fiction of a pure consciousness of the subaltern. Thus, paralleling the colonial situation with the British authorities and the natives, both the French and Indian intellectuals, both the colonizers and the colonized, create or participate in this production of a subaltern who can speak.

There are two intellectuals Spivak quotes to problematize this colonial speech act of the constitution of the subaltern as a speaking subject by saying, "I cannot represent." Foucault and Deleuze say that they cannot speak for the other, which seems like a very critical gesture; they say that the others should speak for themselves. Spivak uses two different notions from two intellectuals to understand what is happening in this context. The first comes from a French philosopher named Pierre Macherey, who was a student of Althusser and an important figure in himself. Spivak draws on Macherey's idea that certain texts, or certain acts of thinking, while speaking, also refuse to say something, do not say something. There is a certain silence, a meaningful silence, namely something that is not said. Something that could be said, something that is there but is not said, something that is refused. This involves silence, not in the sense of the complete absence of words, but logos or words that are absent from the actual expression, text, or statement. It is not hard to find the silence in the current example, because the act is one of refusing to speak, repeating that "I cannot speak for the subaltern, I cannot speak for the prisoners." These texts explicitly refuse to speak in the name of the subaltern because the subaltern can speak for themselves. Spivak uses Macherey to say that the most powerful thing that happens in this statement is a refusal that creates a certain entity precisely by not speaking about it, by refusing to talk about it.

A second idea that Spivak uses in the text is "blankness," which is similar to Macherey's thought. She quotes Derrida, who speaks about a certain blankness, a certain silence that follows any text and in which thinking takes place. This is a process of thinking, a production of discourse, of logos, from which the text follows, which manifests itself in a text but does not enter it. Spivak uses this idea to investigate the words refused by the French intellectuals. She quotes Derrida's idea that at a certain moment, this silence is thinking that is consigned to the other. It is not expressed by the speaking subject, Foucault or Deleuze; it is something that they think, a certain idea that is central to everything they say. It is a source of the production of their whole theory, but it is not articulated or mentioned. It is refused in their own texts. It is consigned to the other, namely the oppressed. The oppressed is the subject who holds the notion, the theory, the logos from which these intellectuals speak yet push away from themselves. They don't take responsibility but consign it to the other, to the oppressed who are supposed to speak for themselves. This is the construction of the other of Europe that Spivak understands as the most pernicious, problematic form of epistemic violence, of imperialist logos or of logos in general.

This act produces two subjects. The first is the other, the prisoners, the masses who can speak for themselves, the women. Within the very discourse of critical thinkers who criticize the figure of the sovereign subject of Europe, Spivak says that this silence of saying "I cannot represent the other" reintroduces the same sovereign subject that they themselves critique. She describes how in this kind of speech act of postcolonial critical thinkers, one will find "lists of self-knowing, politically canny subalterns. The banality of leftist intellectuals lists of self-knowing, politically canny subalterns stands revealed" (275). This list consists of prisoners, homosexuals, women, unemployed people, immigrants, and so forth. Spivak says that, through acts of emancipation and empowerment, the critical intellectual re-creates the old traditional colonial fiction of a sovereign subject in the form of the other. That is the first problematic creation.

The second creation, which goes hand in hand with the first, is the creation of the intellectual themself, namely the European subject, the subject that says, "I cannot speak for the other." It is created in this speech act as invisible, transparent, and able to distance and disempower itself. Spivak calls this creation by negation, in which the intellectual says something

72 | Politics of Not Speaking

like: "I cannot speak for them, it is not my place. They should speak for themselves, I only report. I only describe the situation, but I relinquish agency." Again, these are all gestures of goodwill. Spivak argues that this act obscures the power structure to which these intellectuals belong as well as the responsibility that they still have and hold. She says that it obscures the exploited side of the international division of labor, namely, that these intellectuals belong to a certain place. They are not invisible, they are not transparent, they do have responsibility. They are actors in a system of asymmetrical power in which they stand on the side of the exploiters. Saying "I cannot speak for them" is a means of relinquishing responsibility.

Spivak says that this seemingly empowering act is in fact a reproduction of the same colonial power, creating both the other as the subject and the European subject himself by making him transparent through the illusion that he does not exist. More specifically concerning Foucault, she speaks about how there is a power structure that is being thematized and a power structure that is being silenced. She continues: "Sometimes it seems as if the very brilliance of Foucault's analysis of the centuries of European imperialism produces a miniature version of that heterogeneous phenomenon: management of space—but by doctors; development of administrations—but in the asylums; considerations of the periphery—but in terms of the insane, prisoners and children. The clinic, the asylum, the prison, the university—all seem to be screen-allegories that foreclose a reading of the broader narratives of imperialism" (291). Once again, the imperial, colonial context is being silenced. As discussed earlier, this is Spivak's critique of Foucault, which I now connect to the general theme of rendering something invisible. What is being rendered invisible is the international, namely non-European, power structure. This is the second scene of the production of colonial epistemic violence and violence of discourse. It is produced both in the colonial and postcolonial contexts through the paradoxical act of empowerment, of creating the illusion of the speaking subaltern. In terms of the specific figure of the violence of logos, this entails an act of logoclasm that is masked as logos. This is important in this context because it deals with a criticism of the postcolonial act of logoclasm, an imposed silence, which Spivak says is a continuation of violence. Logoclasm here does not solve the problem, but rather the performance of logoclasm is a continuation of the previous violent discourse.

What alternative does Spivak point toward? She mentions two names, the first being Marx. The entire volume in which this text appears is dedicated to Marxism. Spivak mentions Marx to give an example of an analysis of oppressed groups that she claims does not create the illusion that the subaltern can speak, the illusion that the dispossessed or the oppressed are nonetheless part of logos, do have their place and voice. She speaks about how Marx analyzes the situation of the class of the small peasant proprietor, again as an example of the figure of the subaltern. Marx discusses the situation of the small peasant proprietor without, according to Spivak, creating the illusion or making the claim that they have their own voice in this situation. She argues that Marx rather presents small peasant proprietors as divided, dislocated, disseminated subjects. It is not a sovereign subject that knows itself and speaks for itself; it is still divided. One could use the same adjectives for the word logos: the Tower of Babel, language, discourse that is split, dislocated, divided, dispersed. The small peasant proprietors have no consciousness as such; Spivak says that they cannot represent themselves.

An additional motif that I mention briefly is Spivak's emphasis on the distinction (again a question of translation) within the word "representation." There is a distinction in German between representation as *vertreten* and representation as *darstellen*. Representation as *vertreten* means that "I am now standing and speaking on behalf of one that is not here, the other is absent," while *darstellen* means that "I am speaking to you as the very presence that I embody." Spivak argues that these understandings are opposing notions of representation. Furthermore, she underlines that when critical intellectuals today say that they do not want to represent the other, they mix up absence and presence as if they were the same. Spivak asserts that for Marx, the fact that the small peasant proprietors cannot represent themselves makes them split subjects; they don't even have a consciousness. They cannot be present because they have no consciousness, no identity, and thus mainly have to be represented by something else as an entity that has neither the authority nor the possibility to embody this class, but instead tries to represent its interests. Spivak calls this *vertreten* without *darstellen*. This is the first example that she gives of a different way of approaching, talking about, and politically dealing with the question of a subaltern existence, a position she herself does not espouse. Also in Marx's text, while *vertreten* without *darstellen* is not necessarily a good thing, it is nevertheless a possibility of understanding. Spivak advocates a different theorization, namely Derrida's counter theorization.

As I said from the beginning, Spivak is following Derrida, whom she deploys as a countertheory or strategy to Foucault and Deleuze. She argues that Derrida's entire project, even throughout his deep involvement in the critique of colonialism and Western imperialism, never tries to offer the

74 | Politics of Not Speaking

perspective of the other, never tries to deal directly with the oppressed. She says that Derrida does not provide a program for the oppressed, but rather addresses the benevolent Western intellectual. He undertakes a self-critique of the Western intellectual. Spivak argues that Derrida undertakes a basic endeavor to resist and critique the recognition of the third world through assimilation. She denotes "recognition" with scare quotes. Why? That's the entire problem: recognition is creation. When one recognizes the voice of the other, one creates the fiction that the other has a voice. Spivak argues that Derrida resists and critiques these gestures.

She underlines that "Derrida does not invoke 'letting the other(s) speak for himself'" (294), namely, that he does not invoke this notion, figure, fiction of the subaltern as a sovereign subject. Derrida does not desig-nate it as an autonomous, continuous, wholesome, healthy logos, "but rather invokes an 'appeal' to or 'call' to the 'quite-other' *(tout-autre* as opposed to a self-consolidating other)" (294). Spivak speaks about two figures of the other. There is the other that is created as a fiction, as a subject; and there is what she calls *tout-autre.* The *tout-autre* is the other as an entity that is not an other subject like me, just over there in the prison, in the factory, in India: it is an other in a more radical way. I cannot even conceive of it as a subject. This is the reason for *tout-autre*; there is no act of assimilation, of saying that this other that I will not speak for is nonetheless a speaking subject like me who has their own thing to say. No, I cannot relate to the invocation, the call of the *tout-autre.* Spivak rather calls upon, quoting Derrida, a "rendering *delirious* that interior voice that is the voice of the other in us" (294). This is a key sentence that she quotes twice in this text. She calls upon the *tout-autre* to render *delirious* that interior voice that is the voice of the other in us.

What exactly does she mean by "rendering *delirious* that interior voice that is the voice of the other in us"? The voice of the other in us is pre-cisely this attempt to structure, to construct, the other as a subject like me—which is my own self-constitution as a subject. The complementary tweak is rendering myself invisible by not taking responsibility for this subjectivity and instead ascribing it to the other, the one who speaks; that is, the other in me who is a part of the construction of myself as a self, as a subject. Spivak asserts that the *tout-autre*—namely this discourse that is broken, this humanity that is not a sovereign subject, that does not play the game imposed, that cannot be rendered in terms of a whole, autonomous, reflective, sovereign subject in some way—needs to be encountered such that one does not impose this fiction of sovereign subject of the other in order to construct oneself. Rather, one needs to somehow allow this brokenness, dispersion, split of logos, subaltern condition as such, this inability to speak, this delirium, to open oneself up so as to destabilize the fiction of the sovereign subject within oneself that is ascribed to the other. This is the project that Spivak finds in Derrida.

Lastly, Spivak has another message that needs to be made clear. She asserts that the Western postcolonial intellectual cannot retreat from discourse. In order to really problematize a certain subject, one cannot retreat; one cannot say that they cannot speak and that the other should speak for themself. On the contrary, according to Spivak, the gesture needs to be reversed. The silence, the retreat, the refusal, the transparency, needs to be made visible, namely, the positionality of the speaking intellectual needs to be made manifest. According to her understanding, Foucault and Deleuze need to reflect on their own position. She goes on to say that "there are people whose consciousness we cannot grasp if we close off our benevolence by constructing a homogeneous Other referring only to our own place in the seat of the Same or the Self. Here are subsistence farmers, unorganized peasant labor, the tribals and the communities of zero workers on the street or in the countryside. To confront them is not to represent *(vertreten)* them, but to learn to represent *(darstellen)* ourselves" (288). This intervention needs to take place through the act of rendering one's own subject position visible so as to make visible the kind of discourse one produces, the kind of discourse we produce. "We" in this context refers to Western intellectuals. It is not a counterintuitive retreat but an act of becoming more conscious of the power that we embody and incarnate—*darstellen.*

5

No One Language: Jacques Derrida

Today is our last session in this seminar on the politics of not speaking, which has consisted of a lot of speaking. We will discuss the fifth position in this ongoing investigation of politics and language, "logo-politics" as I call it, or more specifically, the politics of logoclasm, or the break, disruption, or interruption of logos by thinkers in the twentieth century who try to think of politics as a mode of being where logos, discussion, language, communication, and understanding collapse in a radical way. The discussion began with my suggestion of theological beginning with the Tower of Babel, and it moved on to Schmitt's notion of a physical opposition, war, that is an extreme level of intensity of disagreement. It then moved on to Heidegger's idea of the intercultural, interepistemic, or intercivilization encounter; this is where the violence of conversation and discussion entered. In fact, this was already present in Schmitt, but it became more radically conceptualized in Heidegger. The last sessions were devoted to two canonic theoreticians of decolonial and postcolonial thought, Frantz Fanon and Gayatri Spivak, and the more historically concrete stages of colonialism and decolonization.

Our investigation of colonialism was rooted in the idea of this failure or break of logos, logoclasm, in which politics in the broadest sense of the word is constituted. This does not just include politics of institutions, it includes the entire organizational structure of society, the very mode of collective being and existing. This idea is present in Spivak's discussion of the figure of the sovereign subject, who is the figure of what it means to be human. There is an intimate connection between the subject and the logos and Spivak's problematization of this figure through the question of

78 | Politics of Not Speaking

whether the subaltern can speak. Yesterday we talked about how, paradoxically, Spivak does not point to moments of colonialism at its worst in its manifest violence, as perhaps was the case in Fanon's work. She does not point to dehumanization in suppression, oppression, and apartheid; she does so paradoxically in colonialism's seemingly positive performances, its moments of apparent empowerment of the subaltern, native, and colonized in the attempt to construct a figure of the native, of the other, as a sovereign subject to give them space to speak.

Examples of both the colonial abolition of the ritual of sacrificing widows and of postcolonial critical intellectuals who take a step back and make space for the oppressed to speak for themselves offer a notion of a figure with free will. Spivak underlines how these apparently empowering gestures contain violence that is, to some extent, even more fundamental than the violence Fanon describes. Yet, as previously noted, Fanon addressed his text to similar problematics of the native intellectual, namely the endeavors of decolonization he sees as misguided because they subscribe to the logos offered by the colonizers. Thus, Fanon and Spivak have a similar dynamic, but Fanon speaks more directly about physical violence. In this sense he is more similar to Schmitt in regard to both colonial violence and decolonial or anticolonial corrective violence. Spivak speaks on a more structural, epistemic level, similar to Heidegger. In both Heidegger and Spivak, there is emphasis on paradoxical acts that counter acts of harmony, understanding, and dialogue. Both offer theoretical and political interventions at the epistemic level, or at the level of logos, as a corrective or counteraction. Both likewise offer strategies of simultaneous speaking and not speaking. Heidegger does so through the notion of a conversation of silence, with gestures, while Spivak draws on Derrida to focus on the attempt to other the structure of the self, to introduce delirium into the interior discourse of the Western intellectual.

Today's discussion focuses on Derrida. Spivak translated to English *De la grammatologie*, Derrida's first important book. Today I focus on Derrida's later work, namely texts from the mid-nineties and specifically a text called *Monolingualism of the Other: or the Prosthesis of Origin* from 1996, which was translated in 1998.[1] The focus is on the first part of the title, the monolingualism of the other. *Monolingualism of the Other* is a text that furthers the direction, contact, or call of the other that Spivak offered to open in her own text. This does not entail trying to empower the other in an act that projects or constructs the other as a sovereign subject. On the contrary, it tries to deconstruct—this is a Derridean term—the inner structure of Western logos. Deconstructing is a kind of an act of breaking, destructing, destroying, that, for our purposes, is a logoclastic act. I argue that it is a political act or intervention in the same scene already traced by Fanon and Spivak, one that was already hinted and gestured at in Heidegger and Schmitt, namely the colonial situation. Deconstruction is a decolonial gesture.

Monolinguism of the Other is one of Derrida's most accessible texts in terms of the question of readability or comprehensibility of texts that I mentioned yesterday with regard to Spivak. In this text, Derrida speaks about this notion of unreadability. He discusses the difficulties in accessibility, not just as a matter of style, but as a central performance of the text itself, of language. In this text—this is the issue in all his texts in a sense—he makes this point very clearly and connects it to personal experience. It is not the only text in which Derrida speaks about himself, but it is one in which he does it very directly and connects it in an immediate way to his whole philosophical project, how he intervenes in text or discourse.

Monolinguism of the Other revolves around one statement, which is very often the case with Derrida. There is a statement, phrase, or turn of phrase that is offered at the beginning or at some point that in some sense encapsulates the whole text, not just what the text says, but also what the text does. In this text, this is quite obvious from the very beginning. There is one statement that Derrida is making, remaking and remaking, demonstrating, and explaining: "I only have one language and it is not mine." I only have one language. It is not mine. I only have one language. It is not mine. On the first page of the text, Derrida writes:

> Picture this, imagine someone who would cultivate the French language. What is called the French language. Someone whom the French language would cultivate. And who, as a French citizen, would be, moreover, a subject of French culture, as we say. Now suppose, for example, that one day this subject of French culture were to tell you in good French: "I only have one language; it is not mine." Or rather, and better still: I am monolingual. My monolingualism dwells, and I call it my dwelling; it feels like one to me, and I remain in it and inhabit it. It inhabits me. The monolingualism in which I draw my very breath is, for me, my element. Not a natural element, not the transparency of the ether, but an absolute habitat. It is impassible, indisputable, I cannot challenge it except by testifying to its omnipresence in me. It would always have preceded me, It is me. For me, this monolingualism is me. That certainly does not mean to say, and I do not believe that I am some allegorical figure of this animal

80 | Politics of Not Speaking

> or that truth called monolingualism. But I would not be myself outside of it. It constitutes me, it dictates even the ipseity of all things to me, and also prescribes a monastic solitude for me; as if, even before learning to speak, I had been bound by some vows. This inexhaustible solipsism is myself before me. Lastingly. Yet, it will never be mine, this language, the only one I am thus destined to speak, as long as speech is possible for me in life and in death; you see, never will this language be mine. And, truth be told, it never was. (2)

This is how the whole text starts: with a split, interruption, and disturbance inside the structure of the speaking subject. It is about the subject as a speaking subject who has only one language and that language is not his. There is an inner alienation, a fragmentation of the speaking subject. Thus, from the very beginning, the performance is a deconstruction of the sovereign subject through the problematization of its relation logos. The entire text circles around this issue of splitting and fragmentation. From the very beginning, it is a contestation of what Spivak describes as a basic production of the colonial or Western episteme, namely the sovereign subject.

This performance, this split, this break, has two scenes or levels that it is important to understand. First, Derrida speaks about these issues in a specific context and situation. He first delivered this text as a talk at a conference on French speaking, *Francophonie*, outside France, a situation that arises from imperialism, from colonialism. A similar question would exist about speaking English outside England, or Spanish outside Spain, and so forth. The conference was made up of people from different cultures: writers and thinkers who spoke French and belonged to French-speaking cultures that were not French. What does it mean to speak French but not be French? Derrida speaks about the situation of Algerian Jews. He speaks about the effects of French colonialism in Algeria, especially on Jewish society and culture. On this level of the colonial situation, French colonialism in Algeria is a historical phenomenon. On the one hand, there is a testimony to a specific situation that is being addressed, analyzed, verbalized, and problematized, but that is ultimately personal. However, there is also a universal level to what Derrida says. Speech is also something that is broader and concerns all language. It does not only involve Derrida, an Algerian Jew in a colonial situation, who has only one language and it is not his. It is all language, always, of which we have only one and it is never ours.

In his departure from a personal situation that testifies to a broader issue, question, concern, Derrida embodies something in this text. Going back to Spivak, Derrida *stellt sich dar*. As discussed earlier, Spivak argues that the Western intellectual should not represent the subaltern, the other, but rather should represent themselves in the sense of *darstellen*, in the sense of showing, speaking, presencing, representing, and so laying bare or opening up their own position. Derrida does this by looking at himself as a figure, a voice, that testifies to something that is not just individual and personal. It is a kind of self-figuration, what he calls a confession in a religious-theological tone that is never far away. His confession leads him to make bold, daring, provocative statements of exemplarity. He embodies something; he is a paradigm of something.

For example, Derrida states that "According to a circular law with which philosophy is familiar, we will affirm then that the one who is most, most purely, or most rigorously, most essentially, Franco-Maghrebian would allow us to decipher what it is to be Franco-Maghrebian in general" (11). In this context, Derrida speaks about the Franco-Maghrebian context, namely Francophone cultures in North Africa, like Algeria. This involves someone who is paradigmatically Franco-Maghrebian, meaning that if we look at that person, if we identify and contemplate them, they will reveal something more general. He goes on to announce that "We will decipher the essence of the Franco-Maghrebian from the paradigmatic example of the most 'Franco-Maghrebian,' the Franco-Maghrebian par excellence" (11). This statement is an exaggeration, a hyperbole—namely in designating himself as the most Franco-Maghrebian—in order to say something about the situation of speaking French in North Africa. Derrida says something similar in a later passage, but this time not about the French Maghreb, but the French:

> Speak in good French, in pure French, even at the moment of challenging in a million ways everything that is allied to it, and sometimes everything that inhabits it. Without a doubt I contracted this hyperbolism "more French than the French," more "purely French" than was demanded by the purity of purists . . . Excess beyond excess: impregnable. Especially, the same hyperbole will have rushed a French Jewish child from Algeria into feeling, and sometimes calling himself, down to the root of the root, before the root, and in ultra-radicality, more and less French but also more and less Jewish than all the French, al the Jews, and all the Jews of France. And here as well, [more Francophone Maghrebian] than all the Francophone Maghrebians. (49)

82 | Politics of Not Speaking

Derrida enacts exaggeration, an act that presents himself as a paradigm for Jews, for French Jews, for Maghrebians. There is a performance here, the performance of the exemplarity of a subject who is broken, split. "I have only one language and it is not mine." One could also say that it is a testimony of an injured, wounded, suffering subject. I don't say victim. I could, I don't; Derrida doesn't. There is a wound that is being performed, a testimony of suffering that Derrida describes as *martyrium*. In Greek, "martyr" means witness, someone who testifies not just by what they say, but by the suffering that they endure. Here suffering is in language and its splitting.

Q: That is also very Christian again.

A: Indeed, and there is an ambivalence that I will now underline with regard to the role of Christianity in Derrida's thought. The question of Christianity as at the core of Western culture, and also of colonial performance and imperialism, arises explicitly in certain moments in Derrida. On the one hand, Christian discourse lends language to very radical performances and interventions in anticolonial texts, as exemplified by Fanon. Christianity plays an interesting, ambivalent role in such settings, also for Derrida. At some moments in this text, he speaks from a position of a specifically Jewish colonized person in Algeria, and also about what he calls "the Christian contamination." This term describes the contamination of his own Judaism, a colonized situation of Jewishness or Judaism under Christian societies that he doesn't really go into but points toward. At the same time, he himself performs tropes, images, figures, that immediately call to mind Christianity. One can also find this in Judaism, but they have a more dominant role in Christian culture, imagery, or language. It is likewise important to mention that Derrida draws heavily on Levinas, especially in regard to the questions of testimony, martyrium, and ambivalence to Christianity.

Q: There is also the position of Jewish people who were forced to convert to Christianity but maintained Jewish practices. Thus, there is also the figure of the Jew who has Christian language but is also split as a Jewish convert forced into it, not really a Jew anymore, but not really a Christian.

A: Yes, you are absolutely right; we will see that Derrida speaks about this, although primarily about the conversion of Jews into the French state. This idea very clearly echoes the earlier efforts of converting Jews into

No One Language: Jacques Derrida | 83

Christianity, not the modern state but the Christian world and church. Derrida is not the first to point out these ambivalences in the process of Jewish emancipation, which is usually understood as a moment of liberation and so forth, but—as already presented by Fanon—emancipation is itself a problematic word. It means the emancipated, enfranchised slave. In this sense, you could apply the postcolonial, decolonial problematization precisely to this idea of harmony, logos, and the violence in this unity, unification, and liberation. There is a lot to be said, and already has been said, about the way in which Fanon very directly drew on the Jewish experience. Likewise, his teacher, Aimé Césaire, as well as Sartre, drew on the analogy to the situation of the Jews in the formation of decolonial discourse. Here Derrida forms another step in this constellation, one in which Jews are taken as an important figure in understanding the question of colonialism and the problems of decolonialization. Christianity goes deep here.

Q: Does Derrida want to individually separate from Christianity? Does he accept it as his own space?

A: He remains firmly with the statement "I have only one language" until the end. As we will discuss shortly, the specific intervention that Derrida offers is a complex one. What is Derrida's testimony? What does he testify to through this martyrdom that is repeated as a split, a break in logos and language? He testifies to the situation of the disturbance within the subject that is not in full possession of itself, not autonomous or complete. Likewise, its logos and language are not full and complete, but are somehow interrupted; there is disturbance, a break. Concretely, Derrida addresses the historical circumstances of his own upbringing in a Jewish community in colonial Algeria. He speaks concretely about where one sees this split, this wound, in language. He speaks about a triple prohibition on language and speaking; in the terms of our seminar, this involves a politics of not speaking, or colonialism as a politics of prohibition on speaking.

What we discussed earlier in regard to Fanon now appears in Derrida in other terms. Derrida describes the logo-politics of colonialism in Algeria as logoclastic, namely as imposing breaks, negations, and prohibitions on speaking via prohibitions on language, prohibitions on speaking certain languages or all languages. The first of these is the prohibition of non-French languages, described by Derrida as the prohibition of speaking, learning, acquiring, appropriating, and dwelling in non-French languages.

84 | Politics of Not Speaking

This includes non-French Arab or Berber languages in Algeria, the native languages of Algeria and North Africa. Derrida describes how the entire colonial Algerian education system in which he grew up sent a clear message that these were not languages one should know, learn, or speak, although these were the languages spoken by most people in Algeria. Nonetheless, the school, the institute of knowledge, gave a clear message: these are not languages to speak. Derrida speaks about Arabic as the most foreign language for him, the one in which he experiences the most alienation due to this prohibition. At the same time, he says that precisely because of this strong prohibition, it is the language to which he feels the greatest affinity.

The second non-French language that the colonial system prohibits him from speaking, one that is thus negated, broken, is the Jewish language, or Jewish languages in plural. There are many that someone like Derrida could have spoken growing up, including Hebrew, Judeo-Arabic, and Ladino. These are languages that belong to Jewish tradition and culture in Algeria and North Africa. Derrida says that the second prohibition is on these languages, connected to the act of growing up knowing that these are not the languages that he should study, learn, appropriate, and dwell in. Here lies the epistemicide of assimilation. In this context, Derrida provides a testimony of what Fanon calls the native intellectual. He is a North African who grew up in Algeria alienated from his culture; he is taught that in order to be human, to be a part of the world and its order, he needs to not speak Arabic or Jewish languages. He is offered only one language, the language of the metropole, the language of the colonizers: French. This is what a person needs to speak, the only language that one should know to have a place in the world, to succeed. However, it is precisely here that the third prohibition arises, namely the prohibition on all languages.

The first and second prohibitions are on non-French languages; however, the third one is paradoxically a prohibition on the only language Derrida is offered, French. What is the nature of the prohibition on speaking French? It is rooted in the message that "French is the only language for you, but you are not French." Some people can speak French and some people are French. Derrida speaks of the paradigmatic colonial situation in which there is a clear distinction between the metropole versus the colony and its natives who are being educated, colonized, humanized, enlightened, emancipated, taught French. At the same time, they are inscribed in a system in which, structurally, they are never masters in that they are never really French, never the pure French of the metropole, never the French of

France. Derrida describes how such non-French people always have a certain accent; it is always marked, clear. The very language that is given is already marked as a language that they cannot have. This ultimate prohibition on all language, a politics of not speaking, goes back to Derrida's statement: "I have only one language."

Derrida's insistence on this Jewish element, on Jewish belonging, is important. Jews in Algeria were made citizens of France in 1870, but this decree did not include Muslims in Algeria. The Jews were assimilated into the continent and consequentially forced to give up, renounce, their non-French Jewish languages. Derrida says that because of this discrimination, non-Jewish Muslim or Berber natives who were not emancipated were not forced to assimilate and not forced to renounce their own languages. Thus, when Derrida says, "I have only one language," he says it vis à vis the Arab participants at the same conference. They have Arabic and are thus bilingual, but he says that he does not have Jewish languages precisely because of this act of emancipation. As an Algerian Jew he has only one language, but "it is not [his]," because he is not French, but colonized, Algerian. This is the historical context from which this situation arises: "I have only one language and it is not mine." It is the situation of the Algerian Jew, one that Derrida sees as embodying the colonized subject in an exemplary manner.

This manner of understanding colonialism is logoclastic. This is, however, different from Fanon's approach. For Fanon, there is also a prohibition on language in the sense that he depicts the natives as completely, structurally excluded from the order of the world. Derrida says something similar, but in a different way, namely by speaking more specifically about language. This is why he is close to the core of our seminar, the politics of not speaking. Derrida's understanding involves the Jewish Algerian as a figure or martyr who testifies to the general situation of the colonized subject as a prohibited speaker.

Yet, as alluded to earlier, Derrida's idea of testimony works on two levels. In this case, there is a specific testimony about a historical-political situation of the colonized Algerian Jews. However, there is also a general testimony. The Jewish Algerian is a figure for the colonized subject in general, but Derrida also intervenes on a more general level. He offers himself as a witness, a martyr, in the context of the subject, human being, or human existence in general.

For Derrida, the Jewish example provides a paradigm of the colonized; conversely, the situation of the colonized is a paradigm of the human. Note that Derrida intervenes in humanism, in what is human. The colonized, the natives, are not the non-humans, less than humans, dehumanized; they are paradigmatic humans. This is a center of Derrida's text: when he says, "I have only one language; it is not mine," it is the human who speaks. This is true of all language in that it is a split that belongs to the general existence of language. He explains this further, using the colonial situation as a paradigm for the human situation in general. Derrida underlines that "All culture is originarily colonial" (39). Colonialism is not only something that happens in the colonial setting, but also something that happens in human existence, in human society as culture. He goes on to suggest that "in order to recall that, let us not simply rely on etymology" (39). Namely, "culture" and "colonial" come from the same word; "cultivate" and "colonize" come from the same root. Furthermore: "Every culture institutes itself through the unilateral imposition of some "politics" of language. Mastery begins, as we know, through the power of naming, of imposing and legitimating appellations. We know how that went with French in France itself, in revolutionary France as much as, or more than, in monarchical France" (39). Here Derrida refers to the central epistemic project of the French Republic, the normalization of names, measurements, and the metric system. In France there were different regions, localities, accents, languages, measurements, and names that were standardized. Thus, an operation of colonization took place in France itself. Derrida underlines that "This sovereign establishment may be open, legal, armed, or cunning, disguised under alibis of 'universal' humanism, and sometimes of the most generous hospitality. It always follows or precedes culture like its shadow" (39). The text here opens a window to Walter Benjamin's interpretation of culture as oppression, as violence.

Derrida doesn't speak against culture, but he says that mechanisms of colonization can be found in all acts of culture. This is why the situation of the colonized is a paradigm for the human situation in general: the prohibition of language in the colonized situation is a paradigm for the prohibition of language in general. There is a colonialism of culture as such, which consists of homogenization and unification. Derrida argues that these positive acts of politics—particularly the notions of unity, living together, and understanding each other—already enact some violence consisting of homogenization and erasure of difference. This is the same notion of dialogue, conversation, and logos as silencing that we encountered in our earlier discussions.

If the disturbance, interruption, fragmentation, and lack of sovereignty of the split, colonized subject is paradigmatic for the human situation as such under conditions of culture, then we need to reflect on the specificity of colonialism. There are two levels of problematics, the first being the level of culture as colonial per se, as something that erases. Yet there is a more specifically colonial problem, a more specific colonial evil or sin—to briefly refer back to Schmitt and Fanon. The problem or evil of colonialism is neither the splitting of the subject nor the prohibition or fragmentation of language, nor the dispossession of the subject from its own logos. The problem is rather the pathologization of this split. It is the marking, stamping, and branding of the dispossession, lack of control, or fragmentation of one's language as abnormal. Namely, it is the normalization and establishment of an idea of what is normal in relation to which everything else is inferior. This concerns the creation of the figure, figment, and fiction of this split, as if the fragmentation, dispossession, and loss had stemmed from an original state of full possession that exists in Paris, one that could have existed in Algeria for the Jews. As if someone like Derrida, who has one language that is not his, were sick, wounded, suffering. As if there were a wholesome, sovereign subject that he is not, but could have been, namely the French person in Paris, the Algerian before colonialization, or the Jew before emancipation. As if it were colonialism that had created this split and fragmentation. Colonialism, according to Derrida's analysis, introduces this fiction of the normal.

I want to turn to what I call Derrida's confession. Thus far we have dealt with his testimony. Derrida testifies to Jewish, colonial, and human situations. However, he offers more than a testimony; he offers a confession that is a constitutive act of language, that intervenes in the situation. Although I do not say "correct" or "decolonize," what he does is nonetheless similar in the sense that his intervention begins in language, because the essence or the core of the issue is language. Derrida's intervention takes place specifically in a performance of language. It is not the first and only place that he uses the word confession, precisely speaking about himself and developing a narrative, discussing how he speaks, learns, starts, and arrives at a performance of language that is his life's work.

Q: Do you think Derrida is saying that colonialism as a European project uses this linguistic structure as a way to reinforce socioeconomic capitalist projects? Or is it some kind of almost transcendental cause?

88 | Politics of Not Speaking

A: My impression is that Derrida does understand and address the economic problems and power structures that operate on a more physical, material level. Namely, he deals with problems of colonialism such as discrimination and exploitation. Derrida locates or analyzes this by trying to decipher or understand certain mechanisms that work on an epistemic level, similarly to Spivak and Fanon. He portrays a structure in which violence does not only consist of one group forcing another to do something that it doesn't want to do, against the will of the other. Rather, the essence of colonialism, as it also is for Fanon and Spivak, is the epistemic violence of creating a situation in which a group performs its own repression by assimilating itself, appropriating and enacting the colonial repression as if it were emancipation. This is the point in Fanon's critique of the native intellectual, Spivak's critique of subaltern studies, and Derrida's self-reflection or self-contemplation. Derrida is trying to explore the mechanisms of cultural oppression.

I now want to discuss what Derrida calls his confession, this narrative that he develops of a performance in or of language to intervene in the situation he describes. One could call this a decolonial logos and the creation of identity. He even uses this word, calling it the act of telling oneself about oneself: telling one's story, verbalizing and therefore narrating existence and belonging. Derrida chooses his particular location as Jewish from the beginning. He explores a specific position in which Jewish identity and performance in language arise from this disturbed situation of colonial or cultural subjectivity and language. Our discussion concerns the colonial one, which stands for culture. Derrida proposes a strategy, an action that he traces, locates, names, or connects to the Jewish situation, but there is another concept that he uses to characterize this Jewish act of decolonialization within language: the concept of translation.

Gil Anidjar once pointed out to me that we can find a discussion of translation in almost any of Derrida's texts. His first published work was a translation. As I have discussed through other thinkers, translation is a figure of logoclasm, an act in logos of giving voice and silencing at the same time, unconcealing and concealing in the same gesture. Derrida attempts to explain this gesture—in a sense what Spivak called the call to the other to create a delirious state within oneself—in a long footnote about German Jews. He presents a polemics, a conflict, via an opposition within the Jewish colonized subject. He takes the Jewish experience as a paradigmatic experience of being, existing, as a host or guest within another culture, namely as existing in a state of belonging and not belonging at the same time, which he offers as a way of formulating the paradigm of the colonized and the paradigm of the colonizer in general. More specifically, he looks at two models of Jewish response to the situation of split language, of disturbed identity or fragmented subjectivity.

There are two models or forms of Jewish performances in language that try to respond to the colonial situation, and these are two models of translation. The split is between two geographically and otherwise defined Jewish cultures: the Western Ashkenazi, European, inner-European culture, more specifically German Jews, and the Eastern Oriental culture, sometimes called Sephardi. I say this because Sepharad, Spain, goes back to Europe, but for the sake of our discussion it helps to distinguish between Europe and the colonies of Europe, Jews in the continent, in the metropole, in Germany or France, versus the Jews in the colonies of Europe, mainly North Africa.

In this long footnote, Derrida signals a harsh polemic against German Jews. He understands one model of translation as a response to the inner-colonial situation of Europe, namely Jews emancipated and assimilated into German, European culture. Derrida tries to describe and criticize the basic performance of this Ashkenazi model of dealing with the colonial situation through a focus on modern German Jews' immersion into German and total embrace of the German language. They totally embrace German language, emancipation, and assimilation, and thus colonialism, echoing Fanon's native intellectual. Derrida points toward a trend within Ashkenazi German Jews; he does not say all German Jews, but he points toward a trend in prominent German-Jewish thinkers, particularly Franz Rosenzweig and Hannah Arendt. He points out the performance in which both take part: the different, complementary ways in which colonialism is embraced through the embrace of the German language. The German language, and thus language as such, is embraced as one and united, underlining a subject that is in total possession of logos. This concerns not just German, but broader language itself and logos. Derrida points out how both Rosenzweig and Arendt, in complementary ways, articulate a logo-politics that reproduces and reinforces the colonial project of homogenization. He describes this in terms of a translation that has the goal of creating one language, a translation aimed at creating, performing, or manifesting one language.

Derrida first speaks about Franz Rosenzweig, an important German-Jewish thinker, who invested many of his last years in the huge project of translating the Hebrew Bible into German. This was not the first translation ever made

90 | Politics of Not Speaking

of the Hebrew Bible into German; there were many other German translations of the Bible, not least of all by Luther. Rosenzweig and Martin Buber were working together on a translation of the Hebrew Bible into German in the 1920s. Derrida points out that both thinkers aspired to create something that he calls an absolute translation in the sense of a text that no longer looks like translation, but rather a text or translation that becomes original. Buber and Rosenzweig tried to create a biblical German that could, in a sense, become an original, one in which German, the language of translation, would become the original language, while Hebrew would no longer be needed. Such a translation would create one language, namely German.

Derrida then points to a famous interview with Hannah Arendt in the sixties in which she was asked about her experience as an immigrant in the United States. She said that what remained from her lost German past was the language, that German as her mother tongue was something that would always remain. German was a mother tongue that could never be replaced or fully translated, a certain origin that is untranslatable. This is the complementary action between Arendt and Rosenzweig that Derrida points out. Rosenzweig creates a perfect translation of the Hebrew to the German; German becomes the original and is then adopted by Hannah Arendt as something untranslatable. German becomes the only language, the one language, the only, holy one.

Derrida quotes Rosenzweig in one of his texts in which he speaks about how translation is a messianic act that points toward the unity of all languages. Rosenzweig actually says in this text that there is only one language, only one logos. According to Derrida, this is how the colonized adopt and become the executors of the colonial project. He identifies this as one Jewish strategy of dealing with the colonial situation, the German Ashkenazi one. It is appropriated from the colonial project itself, which is a harsh critique and thus relegated to a footnote, but I am now making this footnote the center of the text.

Derrida offers his own polemic against this Ashkenazi German-Jewish performance. At least I interpret Derrida's own act of language as acting against this German-Jewish performance. It is an act of logo-politics that is Algerian, Sephardic, Oriental, or, as we say in Hebrew today, Mizra-chi, meaning Oriental. One could summarize this performance with one sentence: there is never only one language, *il n'y a jamais qu'une langue*. Rosenzweig and the German performance is about there being only one language. Derrida argues that there is never only one language. He mounts his project of language as a logo-political act of resistance to colonialism, which at a certain point he identifies with patriotism. Colonialism and nationalism are similar in this sense; in Derrida's description, colonialism and the creation of the nation-state of France are analogous. Later, Derrida speaks in political, revolutionary terms about what he himself is doing in language: "Compatriots of every country, translator-poets, rebel against patriotism! Do you hear me! Each time I write a word, a word that I love and love to write; in the time of this word, at the instant of a single syllable, the song of this new International awakens in me. I never resist it, I am in the street at its call, even if, apparently, I have been working silently since dawn at my table" (57). Derrida plays with this idea of logo-political intervention in the French language as an act of resistance to national patriotism. In contrast to what Derrida claims Rosenzweig and Arendt are doing, one could call this an act of decolonized French, or decolonizing French. Instead of adopting the colonial notion of the one language, Derrida suggests that, in his forced conscription into the French language, he can generate a counter-act that at a certain moment he calls revenge. He acts on the language, he does something to the language, he makes something happen to the language. He enters into the French language and operates on the French language. He pushes it to its end, he exaggerates, he creates a hyperbolic performance of French normality and purity, a caricature of the idea of French as one pure language. Derrida resists this quest of purity by compulsively dedicating himself to it, by becoming more French than the French. He continues:

> this hyperbolic taste for the purity of language . . . speak in good French, in pure French, even at the moment of challenging in a million ways everything that is allied to it, and sometimes everything that inhabits it. Without a doubt I contracted this hyperbolism ("more French than the French," more "purely French" than was demanded by the purity of purists even while I am from the very beginning attacking purity and purification in general, and of course the "ultras" of Algeria), this intemperate and compulsive extremism, from school, yes, in the different French schools where I have spent my life. (48–49)

Derrida subjects himself completely to the French language's demand for purity. He pushes it, he exaggerates, he creates excess, he becomes a French zealot of the French language. There is a neurosis, which he describes as the neurosis of the Algerian Jew who will never be French, who insists on

92 | Politics of Not Speaking

becoming more French than the French. Someone who insists on purifying his language and arriving at a level of command of the language, of a reflexivity, contemplation, awareness of language that is beyond any doubt of impurity. He calls this being more French than the French: knowing the language and commanding it. What happens is a hyperbolism.

If you know Derrida's text, you can see that the language is absolutely self-reflexive in many moments. Every word that he says immediately follows a reflection on the word (a suggestion of words that are close to it or far from it) and lists of etymologies. There is no longer an immediacy of the subject that simply speaks, who is, who embodies logos. The subject is constantly at a distance from its own language. By the very act of looking for the purity of the perfect possession of the language, a constant break with the language is created. This kind of hyperbolism, excessive control of the language, creates what Derrida calls writing.

Writing here represents the break of the absolute merging of subject and language. The subject who speaks immediately, simply speaks, who is completely immersed with the flow of fluent speech, incarnates logos. Writing breaks from this. The nonimmediate sign becomes a thing alienated from both the subject and its signification, from sense. This is what Derrida calls writing, which is a central notion that he develops throughout his projects. Another way of describing this operation is deconstruction, namely the deconstruction of logos by logos, all the time: a breaking, de-structing. Derrida tries to speak like them, the pure French, but he also constantly questions it. Is it really pure French?

Derrida describes what happens as a model of translation; however, not the German translation that creates or generates homogeneity, unity of language, but a translation that creates the fragmentation and split of language. "I have only one language and it is not mine." It is a split within French, a split of language within French, a split in the French language that Derrida receives from French society as normal, that he questions in a quest for purity, that he questions in light of an imaginary pure French. His performance creates a split between the given and the purist French language. He calls it an inner Franco-French split and names his linguistic performance, his speech-act, an inner Franco-French translation. Through Derrida's insistence, purity, and control, the given French—the French that is being spoken in school, at university, by his colleagues, by other writers, the normal French—becomes derivative. The original French becomes a translation, namely of the more original, more pure French.

No One Language: Jacques Derrida | 93

This is the opposite of Franz Rosenzweig's language of translation, the German that translates Hebrew and is turned into the original. Through this fiction of a purer language, Derrida takes French, which is supposed to be the original, and turns it into a translation, something secondary. It becomes the language of translation. It is the opposite of what Rosenzweig is doing; it is a translation that disunites. It takes what seems like unity and shows it to be fragmented, whereas Rosenzweig took two languages and created one. Secondly, Derrida's performance creates a horizon, a shadow, or a sign for a purer French, a purer French that would be *pré-originaire* or *pré-première*, a language before language, purer than the language that is supposedly the first, namely the given French. It is always before the beginning, namely, it is always beyond the possibility of appropriation. It is always purer than what is given as French. In this sense, it is never absolutely translatable; it is untranslatable, it creates some image, a direction, a horizon of French that is untranslatable to the given French.

What happens here is the opposite of Arendt's idea of a mother tongue. Arendt uses the idea of the non-translatable to articulate German as a language that is pure in itself. Derrida uses the idea of the non-translatable to speak about a relation between two languages, the given and the pure, which can never be abolished. The given, spoken, existing French will never be able to completely arrive at the pure French. There will always be a gap. Derrida calls this horizon of pure French that is never reached and continues to destabilize the normal French the *ailleurs*, the elsewhere of language, the other of language.

It is in this realm that Spivak connects with Derrida. As discussed earlier, Spivak talks about opening up, calling to some other to destabilize, introduce a delirium, render delirious the inner logos. Derrida's text is a concrete performance of such an idea via the act of working from within French and opening it up to an other that is not not-French. This is Derrida's point here: it is not about the Arab, Hebrew, or Greek other, but rather the otherness of French itself. There is a contestation or attempt to deconstruct the very sameness and subjectivity of language from within language itself. In a sense, this is a non-colonial, decolonial performance within French itself. I call this the Derridian logoclasm.

Q: I want to take Derrida's gestures to their limits. He speaks about encountering every culture as formed by acts of civilization and colonization. The attempt to break the ability to speak in any standard cultural way is

94 | Politics of Not Speaking

thus a means of destabilizing culture itself, which means every culture as a culture. He gestures—maybe this is also a messianic thing—to a culture beyond culture, or the possibility of a culture that goes beyond any sort of standardization or homogenization. I know that Derrida is more pointing or gesturing to something than transcending this, but is there a place where he does present a culture beyond culture? If everybody adopts this kind of self-differentiating speech, what kind of speech results from this? What language comes after language?

A: This question is pertinent to the whole set of concepts and moments in Derrida's work. There is vagueness in Derrida in regard to what end he envisions. Do the acts of deconstructing and destabilizing belong to the specific temporality of his own performance to undo one era and open up another? Or do they seek to be this other era, this other mode of being and speaking? I think he is suspicious of the performance of another mode of being. His suspicion is that every time we speak about otherness, we will eventually reinforce the same. I think this is his basic tendency. But his deconstructive performance does sometimes appear as a law, imperative, or mode of being and speaking that is not only a preparation for something else, but the very telos. He does this without saying that it is the messianic moment. You can say that this points to a language beyond language, or to some kind of a messianic otherness, but he doesn't say this. At the center of his act stands deconstruction: writing, splitting, and fragmentation. I think that this ambivalence is inherent. It is the aforementioned Franco-French tension, an inner one that the deconstructive activity opens up. It is an existential mode that Derrida embodies that inherently points to something else, that lives in this expectation, that never does more than that.

Q: I have a question about the formula of the text—"I have only one language and it is not mine"—and the idea of prohibition. At the beginning, there are prohibitions on language. This is especially channeled through Derrida as an Algerian Jew deprived of all languages, even though French is supposedly his language, but he is not allowed to speak French. He performs this gesture of being more French than the French, showing that within logos, through creating this prosthetic origin, this etymological monster, this gap in the language itself. The idea of there being one language and it being not mine is also because French itself is split, right? On the one hand, there is a lack of language, and on the other, an excess of language. Is that a way of getting over this prohibition? Is that what he is trying to do, to lift the prohibition in some sense?

A: We can get theological again. In some places, instead of "prohibition," Derrida says "law." I think that there is a theological undertone and a polemic with Christianity here, especially about the place of law in the human project. I think he searches for ways to look at this prohibition, prevention, or limitation as something that does not need to be problematized and abolished, but as something performed, enacted. In this sense, the acknowledgment of the prohibition, the acknowledgment of the law, reflects a counter-gesture to what he understands as the Christian contamination of the fulfillment and supersession of the law through redemption in love and grace. Derrida doesn't say that here, but he has a very famous text on the Tower of Babel, in which he talks about translation, about Walter Benjamin. I think it's clear to him when he speaks about the prohibition of language that the Babylonian prohibition of language—the "confusion of tongues"—set the entire project of culture, humanity, and politics in motion through a prohibition of the one and only language. There is a biblical element in this, as well as a theological counter-Christian polemics. This entails the idea that prohibition is the law, as well as the project of not trying to abolish it; not trying to create the autonomous subject, but rather a subject who exists in a limited autonomy.

Corollary II

On Jewish-Christian Dialogue

The notion of "dialogue" carries today a clear ethical, moral significance. The notion of dialogue is intimately related to the normative idea of epistemic difference, namely the idea of knowledge, of the practice of knowledge, that resists unity and totality, resists the totalization of knowledge. Dialogue in contemporary discourse stands for difference and pluralism. Dialogue both guarantees and performs pluralism in knowledge. In this sense, dialogue is a logo-epistemic practice that counters other monolithic and totalizing practices, such as monologue, dialectics, or logics.

I suggest thinking about dialogue from the broader perspective of what may be called the contemporary break or rupture of logos. We can talk about a contemporary practice of logoclasm, a normative breaking of logos. I suggest situating the ethico-epistemic question of dialogue within a broader contemporary discourse concerning the practice of ethics, and also the politics of resistance to logos, a resistance to the practice of logos, namely to *logein*—to speaking. It is in this sense that I speak of "not speaking."

Can we speak of dialogue as a practice of not speaking? I do think the notions of dialogue and of dialogical thinking are currently deployed within a logoclastic discourse. Nonetheless, does dialogue really counter *logein*—is *dia-logein* not the very performance and dissemination of logos? And if so, wouldn't dialogue not so much contradict monologue as complement it? Is dialogue really the guarantee of epistemic difference? Wouldn't the existence of dialogue already signify the fundamental overcoming of difference, the reproduction of logos in *dia*-logos? Isn't dialogue the enactment of speaking *as* establishing the coherence of logos, the unity of language? Wouldn't the encounter with real difference, with real alterity—deep epistemic, linguistic,

98 | Politics of Not Speaking

cultural alterity—imply, in contrast, the impossibility of dialogue, the end of speaking? Wouldn't the embrace of epistemic difference require something like not speaking, a practice of silence?

It is with this kind of question that I suggest challenging the notion of "Jewish-Christian dialogue." Is this notion itself dialogical? Is it a part of the dialogue that it designates? Is the notion of Jewish-Christian dialogue expressed by one specific party to the conversation; does it represent the position of one side in this exchange? What would the other side be? Would there be a dialogue with a non-dialogical party? Or perhaps the idea and doctrine of dialogue itself is non-dialogical, insofar as it stands above or below the dialogue, outside of the dialogue, out of the question, as a common notion that unites Jews and Christians, above or below all their differences and disagreements? Would the Jewish-Christian dialogue be another name for the Judeo-Christian monologue?

A non-dialogical, Judeo-Christian way of understanding the notion of Jewish-Christian dialogue would be to say that it designates a pluralistic turn in interreligious relations in general, a turn away from a historical existence of each religion as an isolated, self-contained epistemic system toward a new mode of openness to the religious other.

In contrast, it would be more dialogical to understand the notion of Jewish-Christian dialogue as not designating a reciprocal change in attitude of two already symmetrical parties, Judaism and Christianity, toward each other. Rather, it makes more historical sense to reflect on the idea of Jewish-Christian dialogue as Christian, namely as designating a shift in the attitude of the hegemonic Christian discourse toward its Jewish other, a shift from treating the Jew as a mute, inner trope of a self-contained Christian narrative to recognizing the Jew as a separate, independent, and epistemically different other, who can speak for themself, and with whom there can and should be a dialogue. This project of religious, epistemic recognition of Jewish difference is closely related to the fundamental anti-anti-Semitic revision of the cultural, social, and political attitude of the Christian or post-Christian West toward Jews in the aftermath of the Holocaust.

It is this specifically Christian or Western project of Jewish-Christian dialogue as a pluralistic project that aims at providing recognition to the historically oppressed, epistemic Jewish difference—"Jews should speak for themselves," that I now wish to call into question. I do so by drawing on a fundamental critique of dialogue that I deem central to decolonial and postcolonial discourse. In what follows, I first present this critique of dialogue, and then I reflect on its application to Jewish-Christian dialogue.

I begin with the critique of dialogue in decolonial and postcolonial discourse, or in what we can even call postcolonial critique of decolonial discourse. In both these discourses, dialogue is presented and criticized as a colonial project; in both these discourses the critique calls into question the structural ability of the colonized to take part in the dialogue, their ability to exist in dialogue with the colonizer, namely the ability of the colonized to speak.

For the decolonial version of this position, I turn to Frantz Fanon. Fanon claimed that in the language of the colonizers, in the colonial logos, the colonized are inherently colonized—they can never speak for themselves, that is, the colonized are structurally unable to speak. This was Fanon's historical polemics, not against colonialism, but against all attempts to struggle against colonialism with words, through peaceful dialogue. Fanon asserts that liberation from the pure violence of colonialism can only be attained by the counterviolence of armed struggle that refuses, disrupts, and undoes the entire order of colonial logos: decolonization is not dialogue, it is logoclasm. The agents of this revolutionary logoclasm are not the intellectuals, they are the uneducated people, who have no agency in the colonial discourse, who can't speak.

I turn now to the later, postcolonial critique, which I read in the work of Gayatri Spivak. Spivak's critique of dialogue is more radical than Fanon's and, to a certain extent, even applies to Fanon's own narrative. She accepts Fanon's critique of decolonization in dialogue by stressing that the colonized structurally can't speak. But Spivak goes beyond Fanon in that her critique does not only problematize dialogue under the condition of the colonial logos, which structurally excludes the subaltern as a speaking subject; Spivak more fundamentally problematizes as colonial and Eurocentric the very notion of the speaking subject, namely the sovereign, rational, self-conscious subject who speaks for themself and who is the agent of logos, the party to the dialogue. The very idea of dialogue is colonial. And the greatest colonial violence would lie in making its victims believe they are silenced subjects who should be redeemed and restored to their own, proper, decolonized free speech.

Spivak's argument is specifically postcolonial in that she criticizes colonial logics beyond the colonial state, in the very—Western—idea of logos. The direct addressees of her critique are therefore not, like Fanon's, presumed oppressed colonized subjects; they are anticolonial Western intellectuals. Her message to them is that to counter colonization, they should not call the subaltern to speak for themselves, which is the basic colonizing act; rather

100 | Politics of Not Speaking

Western intellectuals should call into question and undo their own self-perception as sovereign speakers.

I am now problematizing the view whereby, through Jewish-Christian dialogue, the historical Christian hegemony of Western discourse opens itself up to its Jewish other by letting Jews speak for themselves. Having gone through the decolonial and postcolonial critiques of dialogue, the problem can now be formulated as "Can Jews Speak?" In other words, assuming that Jews have been the subaltern of European Christianity, the same subaltern underlying colonialism, would a Christian call to a sovereign Jewish subject to speak for themself, to enter dialogue, not so much break Euro-Christian colonization of Judaism as perfect it, namely by bringing forth a Jew created in the image of the Euro-Christian subject?

For a brief reflection in this direction, I bring Jacques Derrida into the conversation. He portrayed Eurocentric colonialism in logo-political terms as propagating the notion of the sovereign, self-knowing subject who can speak, namely in coherent discourse, in logos—in language that is one, which is the precondition for dialogue. Derrida writes on how French colonialism imposed monolingualism on him as Algerian Jew, by way of emancipation. Against the monolingual subject of Euro-Christian colonialism, Derrida posits not the plurality of language, but the brokenness of language, the logoclastic language of Jewish diaspora: the Jews who can't speak—whose language is not their own.

I conclude with a question: Wouldn't the Jewish-Christian dialogue require the diasporic Jew to become another Jew—to become European, namely sovereign and monolingual? Would the paradigmatic Jewish subject summoned and conjured by the Christian call for dialogue be the Israeli Jew, whose sovereignty would be ultimately attested to by his ability to answer this call for dialogue in the negative?

Not Last Words

In contrast to a common understanding of politics as a domain of speaking, which consists in conversation, exchange of arguments, debate and dialogue, an understanding that harks back to Aristotle's conception of politics as based on logos, the aim of these talks is to reveal an alternative tradition, one that understands politics as the site where logos fails, collapses, breaks—the tradition of politics as logoclasm, politics of not speaking.

These two conceptions of politics are not just alternatives, they are in conflict; and this conflict is not just theoretical, a conflict of concepts, in logos, it is political. It is a logo-political conflict, which is currently acute. I wish to introduce this conflict here at the end of my talks in the form of an objection that has been raised against my endeavor. Even if I have been successful in showing the existence of a tradition of thinking politics as logoclasm, even if I have been able to read a politics of not speaking in various twentieth-century authors, is such a conception a good one? Is it preferable to the understanding of politics as the realm of speaking, of reasoning, as based on the exercise of logos?

The preferability in question is political: it concerns the way we wish to shape human collective existence. According to the objection, the politics of speaking offers a vision of peaceful coexistence, where different people, individuals, and groups are united by a universal reason, a common logos, which enables the regulation of the conflicts of collective living through mutual understanding, without violence. In contrast, the politics of not speaking, of logoclasm, gives us a vision of a human society that is irremediably torn between irreconcilable positions and particular identities, where conflicts may not be resolved amicably, through universal reason, but only through force. This very book, so its critics conclude, shows how the politics of not speaking is a politics of war (see Carl Schmitt) and a

102 | Politics of Not Speaking

politics of violence (see Frantz Fanon). Should we not prefer peace over war, agreement over violence, and, accordingly, the politics of logos over the politics of logoclasm?

Let's talk about talking—why speak of not speaking?

The insight guiding this book does not contest the preferability of peace over war or agreement over violence. What it does contest is the crude identification of peace with logos and war with logoclasm. It turns to authors and texts that recognize the violence that is proper to logos, the destructive power of reason, and identify the exercise of logoclasm, the break of speaking, in countering this violence. My claim is that the site of this interruption of speech is politics.

According to this conception, politics does not begin with the rise of logos, of rational human speech, against animal violence; rather, it begins with the intervention of logoclasm against the violence of logos. This insight does not simply identify logos or reason with violence. Furthermore, it does not negate or dismiss dialogue, nor does it posit politics as the end of all speaking. In fact, logoclasm does not consist in mere negation but in interruption. More precisely, the conception of politics as logoclastic accepts the Aristotelian definition of the human being as speaking, as "possessing logos." However, it also understands the human condition as possessing logos in a structural state of imperfection, incompleteness, finitude. Human being, as finite, is logoclastic. In this situation, the power of pure logos, or the claim to such power of perfect rationality, carries the potential for doing violence to the human condition itself, a potential for destroying speaking altogether. Logoclasm, the politics of not speaking, does not negate logos, it makes it possible.

As a founding myth for the logoclastic origin of politics, I mentioned in the introduction the biblical myth of the Tower of Babel. This story traces the emergence of the political condition, which is a humankind divided into different nations and states, back to a seminal logoclastic event—the scattering of the unity of speech in the confusion of tongues. The disruption is introduced in this myth by an act of divine intervention, a speech act. The disruptive intervention, as much as it is violent, is nonetheless depicted as necessary to prevent a great danger, one that arises from the power of the perfect, universal, one language. The precise nature of the danger is not explained, but its symbol is a tower; and the confusion of tongues does not silence speech; on the contrary it multiplies speaking, just as stopping the building of the tower does not end politics but inaugurates it. Both, speaking and politics, are structurally enabled by logoclasm.

Not Last Words | 103

I introduce here another founding myth, of another Babylonian project, the Talmud. It is an oft-quoted story, commonly read as depicting in narrative form the epistemic constitution of the rabbinic tradition. The story is located in a talmudic section that deals with "violence done with words." It is a scene of disputation concerning a certain ritual question, wherein one rabbi disagrees with all the others. His reasoning is flawless. He answers all their objections, yet they remain unconvinced. It is a scene of perfect logos deployed in an imperfect post-Babel world. Frustrated by the obstinacy of his colleagues, the dissenting rabbi demonstrates the power of his words to make a tree move, a stream of water reverse direction. His speech is divine, and even God's voice intervenes on his behalf and confirms his position. At one moment, the rabbi's powerful words threaten to tear down the walls of the academy. The other rabbis stop and ban him, declaring that truth, the Torah, is "not in heaven."

This is often read as a rejection of religious authority in favor of rational dialogue. Yet it is the dissenting rabbi who incarnates reason, and the drama arises from the failure of dialogue. The power that the majority rabbis embody is not rationality but majority, which signifies not democracy but institution, school, polis. The rabbinic logo-polis, the "house of study," where speaking takes place, is built on the ban of divine, prophetic, namely pure, speech. In biblical Babel, God excluded humanity from perfect logos—in the Babylonian Talmud, humanity excluded God from the logoclastic city, from the politics of not speaking. And God—the Talmud cannot resist telling us—smiled.

This book, which focuses on twentieth-century logo-political theory, introduces the logoclastic conception of politics through the work of Carl Schmitt. Schmitt was a jurist, working with speech in the form of law or norm, just like the rabbis. Law, nomos, is the basic form of speaking that constitutes political existence, such as the state, but also other forms of institutions such as cities or associations. In contrast to other legal thinkers, like Hans Kelsen, Schmitt dismissed the idea that state law, the legal system, features a logical system, a domain of logos, and instead insisted that the authority of the law derives not from reason, but from sovereign decision. Law is logoclastic speech.

Like the myth of Babel, Schmitt argued that the political condition is generated by a fundamental rupture in the pure fabric of social rationality. The power of human reason produces conceptual, ideological, moral positions, which are, however, due to the imperfect finitude of our logical capacity, irreconcilable, just like the disagreement in the talmudic story.

104 | Politics of Not Speaking

When the conflict intensifies, Schmitt claimed, the unreconciled conceptual opposition crystalizes into an ontic one; that is to say, the conflict between ideas becomes a conflict between people, and the struggle for truth transitions into a struggle for existence, which is what happened to the fighting rabbis. The animal that possesses logos, by the very power of its finite reason, exists in a basic state of existential enmity, in war. This is the logoclastic condition of politics.

Schmitt's key observation was that in these conditions, in the political condition of ontic war, the greatest danger is of a specific party to the conflict, who like all parties embodies imperfect, broken logos, nonetheless understanding its position as representing perfect logos and itself as standing for pure and absolute reason. If this happens, then such a party would understand its ontic conflict with the other party not as a conflict between two relative positions, but as a war between logos and antilogos, reason and violence, universalism and particularism, humanity and inhumanity—a war between good and evil. In a logoclastic condition, to claim the cause of logos consequently would be to produce a war against an opponent that represented not just opposition, but evil. War against evil is a war against war, a holy war, which aims not just at subduing, but at exterminating the enemy, as absolute, as the enemy of mankind. Preventing holy war of extermination, according to Schmitt's insight, is the logoclastic telos of politics.

According to Schmitt, this was the greatest civilizational achievement of modern Europe, through the political model of the territorially limited sovereign state, in the aftermath of the wars of religion. The secular state's absolute sovereignty means that it is committed to no logos, no reason, no truth—no God. In this sense, the state is the absolute interruption of rationality, the embodiment of pure violence, indeed, as Hobbes depicted it, a Leviathan. Yet the state's power is limited to its territory. Consequently, according to Schmitt's reasoning, whatever reasons drive state violence, economical, national, geopolitical, it never stands for universal logos but always for limited, finite interests. It follows, and this is the main point, that wars between European states are never holy; states are never absolute enemies to each other, only relative and occasional, hence Europe's civilizational invention, the international, interstate law, which regulates, limits, "hedges," war. European laws of war, Schmitt argued, are designed to ensure that a state's war against another state is never a war of good against evil, that European wars are never exterminatory.

What went wrong, according to Schmitt, was the violent reemergence of pure logos in the seminal incarnation of modern woke, the

Enlightenment. Revolutionaries and anarchists recognized the logoclastic essence of the state and waged their war against it in the name of universal reason. More dangerous, however, according to Schmitt, were the liberals, who believed the European state to already *be* the embodiment of reason and to stand for universal humanism, democracy, and rational discussion. Liberalism sanctified the European state as the polis of logos, where politics is free speech and law rules as a coherent system of norms. The liberally minded state, according to Schmitt, consequently wields its unlimited Leviathanic violence, not just in the name of its own limited territorial interests, but in the name of humanity and goodness. It is the cause of universal logos that transformed the limited European states into imperial superpowers and hedged European armed conflicts into world wars.

I think we must call into question Schmitt's claim that the pure violence of the state's sovereign and the pure logos of humanism are contradictory and consider seeing them as two sides of the same situation, namely as two sides of one and the same border. The key lies in understanding the territorial delineation of the state, the border, not as the limitation of its power, but rather as an effect or device of the unlimited character of sovereign might—of the Leviathan. Ultimate power generates its own justification, and the self-justification of state sovereignty is generated by the border. The territorial border has never limited the actual scope of state power. After all, the main institution of sovereign violence, the military, is designed to exercise power outside the state borders. What the border does do is split state power, split the state being, into two regimes, two separate worlds: the inside and the outside. The inner space of the European state is a state of law, a polis of logos, of democracy and human rights. The outer space is a state of war, a world of sovereign, namely absolute, violence.

Both spaces, both regimes, belong to the same sovereign power. This power manifests itself in its ability (technological, psychological, moral, theoretical) to create and maintain the border, to identify itself with the "inside," the state of law, and to deploy its sovereign violence "outside," in war. The state of law and democracy is not an illusion or a mischaracterization, as Schmitt argued. Europe's state power manifests itself in its ability to maintain liberalism (the politics of speaking) as a reality—within state borders. It is precisely as real that the polis of logos, namely the European democracy of human rights, can perform the function that Schmitt recognized of humanism, namely the justification of unlimited state violence in the outside world, beyond law and logos. The inside justifies the outside, democracy justifies war, the politics of speaking justifies the politics of forcing. The greater the state power, the better it separates the inside from the outside, and the more invisible their unity becomes. The greater the distance between state logos and state violence, between civilian and soldier, and the less the former even knows of the latter's doing, the better it justifies it. And just war, as Schmitt noted, is a war of extermination.

The territorial sovereign state thus features a mechanism that produces extermination by justifying pure violence through pure reason. This mechanism also functions in interstate conflicts, notwithstanding the "hedging" device of international laws of war. As Schmitt indicated, the purpose of these laws was to normalize the state of war, to legitimize state violence, and so to prevent a warring state from considering itself good and its enemy evil—to prevent just and so exterminatory war. Yet international laws of war, which exclude the moralization of war, themselves become the marker of absolute morality, such that the alleged violation of these laws, the war crime, emerges as absolute evil, which in its turn justifies the liberal state in waging a total war against the very existence of its enemy.

Justifying state power through the mechanism of a border between inner humanism and outer violence is much more effective when the border does not just divide between one sovereign state and another but between the state and stateless actors. The stateless are placed in the outside space of war, but without any legitimacy to exercise violence like a sovereign state. The stateless are subjected to the lawless, speechless mercy of the sovereign. They are exposed to the brutal reality of the state, which keeps itself invisible to its citizens. To be sure, the border between the citizen and the stateless is not territorial in nature, just as the territorial border is not determined by territory but by the sovereign split between inside and outside. The geographical, spatial, physical separation is not the cause but the effect of this split. But the split between insider and outsider, with its effects of physical separation, often takes place or is actively produced inside the state's sovereign territory by creating different classes of people, different races, who become subject to the state's two separate regimes—logos and anti-logos, speaking and forcing, the former justifying the latter. The Holocaust began in the land of *Aufklärung* through the state racially segregating its own population before sending the excluded Jews physically outside to "the East."

The most durable, however, has been the border between the European state and the non-European world. The great geographical distance between the colony and the metropole made it possible to keep a European world of universal human rights and parliamentary politics apart from a colonial world of apartheid, slavery, and genocides, the former motivating the latter, both ruled by the same sovereign state. Here too, it was not the citizens of the metropole but the colonized who encountered the Leviathan and recognized its border operation. Frantz Fanon described the pure violence of the colonial system, which generates a Manichean reality, split between colonizers and colonized, sons of light and sons of darkness, masters and damned. Aimé Césaire, in *Discourse on Colonialism* (1955), showed how the profound, ontic, racial separation was produced by and in the name of European science, how the reign of violence was justified by the reign of logos. It is crucial to see how the state's unlimited violence in the colony, through enslavement, dispossession, exploitation, and massacres, materially enabled the territorially limited reign of universal rights "inside" the state and also enabled the maintenance of the invisible border over decades and centuries so as to reinforce and reproduce reason on one side and oppression on the other.

Fanon understood that the cause of universal reason, the politics of speaking, had become the ideology of colonizing violence, and that decolonization therefore could not use it but must instead refuse it, refute it, resist it. The seminal act of refutation consists in revealing the structural connection between the humanistic logos of the European state and its colonial violence, in revealing the violence of logos. The revelation requires undoing the border between the democratic inside and the martial outside, which is done by rendering visible the very existence of the border, namely by unveiling the limited, imperfect nature of state reason, by revealing the state itself as a violent disruption of speaking, as logoclasm.

Speaking for the colonized, Fanon argued that their only way to counter colonial violence was through counter-violence since reason itself—discourse, knowledge, laws, institutions—had been colonized. Violence breaks colonial logic. The main point here is that decolonial violence does not primarily aim at defeating colonial violence. Armed resistance may of course critically harm and unsettle the colonizer's forces and ultimately cause its retreat. But the crucial moment is the very eruption of anticolonial violence. For Fanon, this is a moment of liberation, a cathartic recreation of the fundamental agency, subjectivity, humanity, of the colonized, of their ability to speak. Counterviolence is the reentrance of the oppressed into the realm of logos. But the violence committed by the colonized has another effect, almost the opposite. Anticolonial violence disrupts the colonizer's peace and thus breaches and reveals the border between violence and speech, brings violence into the polis of logos, and unveils the prevalent universal logoclasm. In other words, the primary goal of anticolonial

108 | Politics of Not Speaking

violence is not to defeat colonial violence, but to defeat the pretense of logos that justifies it.

The primary epistemic function of decolonial counterviolence is captured by its common designation through the colonizing powers—terror. Decolonial counterviolence exposes state citizens to the unlimited violence that their state signifies outside its borders and shatters their sense of living in a city of pure reason. This is why armed decolonial resistance aspires to hit the colonizing power as much as possible inside its borders, to disturb as deeply as possible its inner peace, the ultimate target being not the solider but the civilian, who is also—on the outer side of the border—the target of colonial violence. The distinction and physical separation between civilians and soldiers, which has become synonymous with morality, in reality arises from the supreme sovereign power that is able to disassociate speaking from weapons. This split, as a phenomenon of the border, produces the humanist civilian society that justifies its own military power, and condemns the violence of non-state anticolonial resistance as terrorism. Note that international law condemns decolonial violence, not because it targets civilians, but because it is carried out by civilians, who are by definition illegal combatants. Since the separation between civilians and soldiers is a privilege of sovereign power, international law in fact outlaws the violence of the weak. Consequently, decolonial counterviolence, branded terrorism, is condemned as a moral sin, as evil. The war on terror is waged as a holy war, a war of extermination, whose goal is not to defeat the enemy but to physically eradicate it. In the tragedy of its ruthless suppression, decolonial violence achieves the goal of revealing the Leviathan, of unveiling the unlimited violence that sustains state reason and justifies itself through it.

The revelation of the state's violence to its own citizens unsettles the border and undermines the mechanism that justifies war by logos. The inner disruption of European reason has played a critical role in the process of post-WWII decolonization. The eruption of violence in anticolonial wars should be considered against the background of the profound internal disintegration of European moral self-consciousness by the logoclastic apocalypse of the two world wars and the Holocaust.

The inner disruption of European logos also manifested itself in the emergence of critical logoclastic thought, such as in the case of the authors discussed in this book. If Fanon followed the insight that the decolonized could only counter the violence of colonial logos through the deployment of anticolonial violence, Heidegger, Spivak, and Derrida offered logoclastic interventions within European discourse, turning Western philosophy against itself. As conceptual operations, as acts of speaking and writing, these interventions do not simply aim at negating logos and universal reason. On the contrary, they aim at salvaging the human project of logos by dispelling the fiction of its Western completion, by deconstructing Europe's own Tower of Babel.

I wish to conclude with a short reflection on the current logo-political predicament. One paradigmatic event of our time is the extreme eruption of violence since the Hamas attacks on Israel on October 7 and the IDF's still ongoing offensive on Gaza in response. The logoclastic perspective on politics, as developed in this book and reiterated in the conclusion, enables perception of the logic of destruction in the unfolding drama.

In contrast to any Western temptation to understand the bloodshed as arising primarily from the conflict between two oriental cultures, the conflict lends itself to a straightforward analysis as exemplifying the logo-political mechanism of the European sovereign state. At the center stands the operation of bordering. The State of Israel is based on the principle of Jewish sovereignty, and accordingly since its inception it has been engaged in producing a border in various ways, a distinction and separation within the population under its power, between Jews, who mark the inside of the state, and Arabs, who mark the outside. Considering that the area in question is small and densely populated by a diversity of populations that coexist in great proximity, producing the separation has required significant resources—technological, economical, ideological, and military. A clear feature of the segregation is that it constitutes the inside Jewish space of the state as a polity of speaking, ruled by democracy, and the outside Arab space as a polity of violence, ruled by police and military. As a common saying goes, the State of Israel, both Jewish and democratic, is democratic for Jews and Jewish for Arabs. The former (Jews as democrats) justifies the latter (Arab subject to Jews).

The most effective separation has been the territorial split between the State of Israel and the Palestinian territories in the West Bank and Gaza since 1967. As Ariella Azoulay and Adi Ophir wrote in *The One-State Condition* (2012), the two sides of the border (what is today called the Separation Fence) are ruled by "two apparatuses in the service of one and the same regime" (1) or, I would say, by two regimes in the service of one and the same sovereign. It has been the same sovereign exercising power on one side of the border in the form of a democratic state and on the other side of the border in the form of military occupation. The democratic apparatus on the Israeli side of the border, the notion that Israel is the only democracy

110 | Politics of Not Speaking

in the Middle East, has not been perceived as standing in contradiction to the rule of violence over the Palestinian side. On the contrary, democracy has legitimized the occupation and the growing dispossession.

The better, more efficient, and more hermetic the separation between Israeli and Palestinian subjects of the sovereign, between logos and violence, namely the more invisible their actual political unity becomes, the easier it is to deploy violence and to justify it. Accordingly, the creation of the Palestinian Authority in 1994 did not reduce but increased the exposure of Palestinians to Israeli military power, which could now more easily deem them foreign to the state. The unilateral "disengagement" of Israel from the Gaza Strip in 2005 thus enabled the designation of Gaza as a "hostile entity" and the imposition of a blockade since 2007.

The Palestinian struggle aimed at breaching the separation by reconnecting the democratic regime to the military one, by unveiling the violence at the heart of logos. I have analyzed the BDS campaign as a logoclastic operation that interrupts the normalizing effect of dialogue by deploying politics of not speaking. Palestinian armed struggle exemplifies decolonial counterviolence insofar as its immediate telos is not to defeat the military power of the IDF but to defeat the democratic peace of mind that this military power enables on the Israeli, Jewish, inner side of the separation. It does violence to reveal violence, it breaches the wall to make the wall visible. Palestinian attacks brought military violence back to the civilian center of Israel—they instilled terror. As terror, Palestinian counterviolence against the State of Israel has always been demonized as moral evil such that the struggle against it did not aim at defeating but at eradicating it.

The Hamas attacks on October 7 physically destroyed the fence between Gaza and Israel, and by their scope and ruthlessness exposed Israelis to the kind of indiscriminate violence that the entire state mechanism is designed to keep outside the border, on the Palestinian side. For hours, the state disappeared, and the horrific reign of violence, the realm of the Leviathan, emerged as a real apocalypse. The Israeli response consequently manifested the fundamental contours of sovereign violence: exterminatory destruction generated by absolute self-justification, driven by the logic of holy war—good versus evil. The extreme evilness of Hamas, which justifies the unprecedented decimation of Gaza, is derived from qualifying their violence not just as terrorist, but as anti-Semitic, as Nazi. The logo-political specificity of this operation consists in inverting the semantic of decolonization. As I noted, the genocide committed by a European state against the Jews, the Holocaust, was a historical disruption of European state reason. In using the Holocaust to justify the destruction of Gaza, the State of

Israel—alongside other Western states—appropriates the collapse of European sovereign logos to restore sovereignty to its unlimited power.

This leads me to a last reflection on the current logo-political configuration. The inversion of the meaning of the Holocaust from critique of state violence to its justification points to a postcolonial condition in which the very discourse that has disrupted the coherence of Western reason becomes one of its pillars: logoclasm turned into counter-logos, which holds the same destructive potential as logos. The struggle against anti-Semitism, which unsettled the self-righteous consciousness of European humanism by unveiling its racism, is now mobilized to edify European state reason and to vilify its minorities. Similar transformations take place in decolonial discourse, which has entered the centers of knowledge production in Western societies, the power plants of Western logos, such that its disruptive function is no longer obvious. Similarly to anti-anti-Semitism, anti-colonialism too, instead of unsettling the purity of Western conscience, becomes a powerful tool for generating a perfect logos of absolute humanity that condemns its enemies as evil and unleashes holy wars. This is a danger that should be considered in countering the Israeli genocide narrative with a Palestinian genocide, or by depicting the Hamas attacks on October 7 as a ghetto uprising instead of as a pogrom.

More generally speaking, the transformation of logoclasm to perfect logos as counter-logos is a basic dynamic in contemporary logo-politics. Twentieth-century disruption of pure reason, the critique of European Enlightenment, did not produce, as it is sometimes claimed, a post-truth era, where imperfect logos relativizes absolute positions, as Schmitt argued the sovereign state was doing. On the contrary, the collapse of instituted reason multiplied the absolutes and rendered truth immediate and omnipresent. This is analogous to Lacan's claim that the death of God did not abolish morality but on the contrary generated absolute moralism, which did not make everything permissible, but rather prohibited. Contemporary truth, as a social production, now enacted in the split spaces of social media, tends to emancipate itself from institutions, from knowledge, from logos, and attach itself exclusively to the immediate evidence of image, affect, and pain such that violence ultimately emerges as the only non-virtual reality. The disruption of Western logos paradoxically operates as its perfection. Rather than post-truth, our time should perhaps be better characterized by post-logos truth and the collapse of politics into morality.

To restore politics as the prevention of holy war, current logo-political interventions should therefore be wary of both the simple assertion of rational discussion against violence and the simple assertion of violence against dialogue. Logoclastic action, disrupting the fiction of pure reason, should not be taken with a view to precluding logos, which amounts to the same absolute truth as its perfection, but with a view to maintaining logos in the state of imperfection, which is the sole way of rendering it humanly possible.

Notes

Chapter 1

1. Carl Schmitt, *Der Begriff des Politischen. Text von 1932 mit einem Vorwort und drei Corollarien* (Berlin: Duncker & Humblot, 2009 [1932]); trans. Georg Schwab as *The Concept of the Political* (Chicago: University of Chicago Press, 2007 [1996]). The references in the present chapter are to the English edition.

2. Carl Schmitt, *Politische Theologie. Vier Kapitel zur Lehre von der Souveränität* (Berlin: Duncker & Humbolt, 2009 [1922]); trans. George Schwab as *Political Theology: Four Chapters on the Concept of Sovereignty* (Chicago: University of Chicago Press, 2005 [1985]). The translations in the present chapter are mine, and the references are to the German edition above.

Chapter 2

1. Martin Heidegger, *"Aus einem Gespräch von der Sprache. Zwischen einem Japaner und einem Fragenden," Unterwegs zur Sprache* (Stuttgart: Klett-Cotta, 2003 [1959]), 84–155; trans. Peter Hertz as "A Dialogue on Language between a Japanese and an Inquirer," in *On the Way to Language* (New York: Harper & Row, 1971), 1–54. The references below are to the English edition.

Chapter 3

1. Frantz Fanon, « De la violence », *Les damnés de la terre* (Paris: La découverte, 2002 [1961]), 37–103, trans. Constance Farrington as « Concerning Violence », in *The Wretched of the Earth* (New York: Grove Press, 1963), 35–106. The references below are to the English edition.

Corollary I

1. Omar Barghouti, *BDS: Boycott, Divestment, Sanctions. The Global Struggle for Palestinian Rights* (Chicago, IL: Haymarket Books, 2011).

2. This goes beyond the defense of academia as transcending politics altogether, and the appropriate response that scientific research has been playing a central role in maintaining the various oppression mechanisms deployed by the Israeli state.

Chapter 4

1. Gayatri Chakravorty Spivak, "Can the Subaltern Speak?," in *Marxism and the Interpretation of Culture*, ed. Cary Nelson and Lawrence Grossberg (Urbana: University of Illinois Press, 1988), 271–313.

Chapter 5

1. Jacques Derrida, *Le monolinguisme de l'autre* (Paris: Galilée, 1996); trans. Patrick Mensah as *Monolingualism of the Other* (Stanford: Stanford University Press, 1998). The references below are to the English edition.

References

Azoulay, Ariella, and Adi Ophir. 2012. *The One-State Condition: Occupation and Democracy in Israel/Palestine*. Stanford: Stanford University Press.

Barghouti, Omar. 2011. *BDS: Boycott, Divestment, Sanctions: The Global Struggle for Palestinian Rights*. Chicago, IL: Haymarket Books.

Derrida, Jacques. 1996. *Le monolinguisme de l'autre*. Paris: Galilée. Translated by Patrick Mensah as *Monolingualism of the Other*. Stanford: Stanford University Press, 1998.

Fanon, Frantz. 2002 [1961]. "De la violence." In *Les damnés de la terre*, 37–103. Paris: La découverte. Translated by Constance Farrington as "Concerning Violence," 35–106. In *The Wretched of the Earth*. New York: Grove Press, 1963.

Heidegger, Martin. 2003 [1959]. "Aus einem Gespräch von der Sprache. Zwischen einem Japaner und einem Fragenden." In *Unterwegs zur Sprache*, 84–155. Stuttgart: Klett-Cotta. Translated by Peter Hertz as "A Dialogue on Language between a Japanese and an Inquirer." In *On the Way to Language*, 1–54. New York: Harper & Row, 1971.

Schmitt, Carl. 2009 [1932]. *Der Begriff des Politischen. Text von 1932 mit einem Vorwort und drei Corollarien*. Berlin: Duncker & Humbolt. Translated by Georg Schwab as *The Concept of the Political*. Chicago: University of Chicago Press, 2007 [1996].

Schmitt, Carl. 2009 [1922]. *Politische Theologie. Vier Kapitel zur Lehre von der Souveränität*. Berlin: Duncker & Humbolt. Translated by George Schwab as *Political Theology: Four Chapters on the Concept of Sovereignty*. Chicago: University of Chicago, 2005 [1985].

Spivak, Gayatri Chakravorty. 1988. "Can the Subaltern Speak?" In *Marxism and the Interpretation of Culture*, edited by Cary Nelson and Lawrence Grossberg, 271–313. Urbana: University of Illinois Press.

Index

Africa, 49, 81
   African, 49, 50, 51
Algeria, 38, 43, 80, 81, 82, 83, 84,
    85, 87, 91
   Algerian war of Independence, 37
Althusser, 70
anarchism, 7, 8, 9, 10
Anidjar, 88
anticolonial, 38, 54, 55, 6, 78, 82, 99,
    107, 108
anti-Semitism, 4, 111
   anti-Semitic, 18, 98, 110
apartheid, 40, 41, 54, 78, 106
apocalypse, 108, 110
appeasement, 43
Arabic, 84, 85
Arendt, Hannah, 89, 90, 91, 93
Aristotle, 2, 3, 101
armed struggle, 38, 49, 55, 99, 110
Ashkenazi, 89, 90
assimilation, 43, 74, 84, 89
Augustine, 39
Azoulay, Ariella, 109, 115

Babylonian, 95, 103
Barghouti, Omar, 54, 55, 56, 114,
   115
BDS, 53, 54, 55, 56, 57, 110, 114,
   115

Benjamin, Walter, 86, 95
Berber, 84, 85
Bible, 3, 24, 89, 90
Black Panthers, 37
blockade, 110
Boycott, 53, 56, 114, 115
   boycotting, 3
Buber, Martin, 90

Catholic, 10
Césaire, Aimé, 48, 83, 107
   Discourse on Colonialism, 107
Christianity, 31, 33, 39, 82, 83, 95,
    98, 100
   Christian, 10, 22, 39, 44, 82, 83,
     95, 97, 98, 100
colonialism, 4, 11, 18, 33, 36, 37, 38,
    39, 40, 42, 43, 44, 47, 50, 5, 6,
    62, 63, 67, 68, 73, 77, 78, 80,
    83, 85, 86, 87, 88, 89, 90, 91,
    99, 100, 111
   colonial, 4, 37, 38, 39, 40, 41, 42,
     43, 44, 45, 46, 47, 51, 54, 55,
     56, 6, 61, 62, 64, 65, 66, 67, 68,
     69, 70, 71, 72, 78, 79, 80, 82,
     83, 84, 86, 87, 88, 89, 90, 91,
     93, 99, 106, 107, 108
   colonizer, 47, 49, 6, 67, 69, 70, 89,
     99, 107

118 | Index

Count Shuzo Kuki, 22, 24

Dasein, 22, 45
de Sousa Santos, 64
decolonialism, 4
Deconstruction, 79
Deleuze, Gilles, 69, 70, 71, 73, 75
democracy, 2, 7, 105, 109, 110
Derrida, Jacques, 4, 61, 66, 71, 73,
    74, 75, 77, 78, 79, 80, 81, 82,
    83, 84, 85, 86, 87, 88, 89, 90,
    91, 92, 93, 94, 95, 100, 108,
    114, 115
  De la grammatologie, 78
  Monolingualism of the Other, 78,
    114, 115
dialogue, 2, 12, 19, 20, 21, 23, 24,
    25, 26, 27, 28, 29, 30, 32, 33,
    35, 36, 42, 44, 48, 53, 54, 55,
    57, 5, 6, 62, 78, 86, 97, 98, 99,
    100, 101, 102, 103, 110, 112
diaspora, 54, 100
documenta, 4

emancipation, 43, 66, 67, 71, 83, 85,
    87, 88, 89, 100
enemy, 6, 11, 13, 14, 28, 41, 48, 54,
    62, 63, 104, 106, 108
Enlightenment, 111
episteme, 4, 61, 62, 63, 80
  epistemic violence, 69
  epistemic difference, 4, 19, 97, 98
  epistemicide, 64, 84
  epistemological, 13
  epistemology, 13
eschatology, 24, 36, 45, 50
European, 11, 18, 22, 23, 26, 27, 28,
    29, 31, 32, 36, 37, 40, 41, 46,
    50, 5, 61, 63, 64, 66, 67, 68, 71,
    72, 87, 89, 100, 104, 105, 106,
    107, 108, 109, 110, 111

evil, 9, 10, 11, 15, 16, 39, 40, 41,
    42, 45, 46, 47, 48, 49, 50, 6, 87,
    104, 106, 108, 110, 111

Fanon, Frantz, 4, 35, 36, 37, 38, 39,
    40, 41, 42, 43, 44, 45, 46, 47,
    48, 49, 50, 51, 52, 54, 55, 56,
    57, 6, 62, 63, 64, 65, 70, 77, 78,
    79, 82, 83, 84, 85, 87, 88, 89,
    99, 102, 107, 108, 113, 115
  Black Skins White Masks, 40
  The Wretched of the Earth, 37, 113,
    115
Foucault, Michel, 61, 62, 63, 69, 70,
    71, 72, 73, 75
  Power/Knowledge, 62
France, 17, 51, 80, 81, 85, 86, 89, 91
Franco-Maghrebian, 81

Gaza, 54, 109, 110
genocide, 64, 110, 111
Germany, 4, 5, 17, 89
Global South, 4, 64
Gramsci, Antonio, 65
Greek, 1, 4, 7, 24, 62, 82, 93

Hamas, 109, 110, 111
Hamlet, 21
Hebrew, 84, 89, 90, 93
hegemony, 65, 100
Heidegger, Martin, 4, 5, 15, 17, 18,
    19, 20, 21, 22, 23, 24, 25, 26,
    27, 28, 29, 30, 31, 32, 33, 35,
    36, 37, 38, 41, 42, 45, 50, 5,
    61, 62, 64, 66, 77, 78, 79, 108,
    113, 115
  Letter on Humanism, 25
  The Black Notebooks, 18
hermeneutics, 31, 32
Hertz, Peter, 19, 21, 113, 115
Hobbes, 104

Index | 119

Holocaust, 98, 106, 108, 110, 111
Human Rights, 53
humanism, 11, 41, 63, 66, 86, 105, 106, 111

Iki, 24, 26
imperialism, 11, 18, 61, 63, 67, 72, 73, 80, 82
India, 64, 66, 67, 70, 74
intercultural, 19, 20, 23, 24, 25, 29, 33, 35, 36, 77
inter-epistemic, 19
International Court of Justice, 56
international law, 12, 56, 57, 108
international politics, 11
Islamic, 4, 22
Israel, 4, 53, 54, 55, 56, 57, 109, 110, 111, 115
  Israeli, 40, 53, 54, 55, 56, 57, 100, 109, 110, 111, 114
  State of Israel, 109

Japanese, 19, 22, 23, 24, 25, 26, 27, 28, 29, 30, 31, 32, 36, 42, 64, 113, 115
Jewish, 4, 22, 43, 80, 81, 82, 83, 84, 85, 87, 88, 89, 90, 97, 98, 100, 109, 110
  Jewish-Christian, 98
Jews, 4, 18, 80, 81, 82, 83, 85, 87, 88, 89, 98, 100, 106, 109, 110
Judaism, 82, 98, 100
Judeo-Arabic, 84

Kant, Immanuel, 21
Kelsen, Hans, 8, 103
Kierkegaard, Søren, 15
Kyoto, 24

Lacan, Jacques, 111
Ladino, 84

language, 1, 2, 3, 5, 6, 7, 12, 14, 17, 18, 19, 20, 21, 22, 23, 24, 25, 26, 27, 28, 29, 30, 31, 32, 35, 36, 37, 44, 45, 46, 51, 5, 6, 61, 62, 64, 65, 66, 73, 77, 79, 80, 82, 83, 84, 85, 86, 87, 88, 89, 90, 91, 92, 93, 94, 95, 97, 99, 100, 102
Leviathan, 104, 105, 107, 108, 110
liberalism, 7, 8, 9, 10, 12, 105
logein, 1, 2, 97
logoclasm, 3, 15, 17, 21, 35, 49, 54, 57, 5, 6, 69, 72, 77, 88, 93, 97, 99, 101, 102, 107, 111
logo-politics, 1, 77
logos, 1, 2, 3, 5, 7, 8, 9, 11, 14, 15, 17, 19, 20, 21, 22, 23, 24, 26, 28, 32, 35, 36, 37, 38, 42, 43, 44, 49, 51, 54, 55, 56, 57, 59, 60, 62, 64, 66, 67, 68, 70, 71, 72, 73, 74, 75, 77, 78, 80, 83, 86, 87, 88, 89, 90, 92, 93, 94, 97, 99, 100, 101, 102, 103, 104, 105, 106, 107, 108, 109, 110, 111, 112

Macherey, Pierre, 70, 71
Manichaeism, 39
Manichean, 39, 41, 42, 44, 47, 50, 56, 6, 107
Mao, Zedong, 46
Maoism, 46
Martinique, 37, 48
Marx, Karl, 45, 46, 51, 65, 72, 73
messianism, 33
metaphysics, 26, 31, 32, 37, 64
Middle East, 110
modernity, 7
mother tongue, 90
Muslim, 85
myth, 3, 10, 102, 103

120 | Index

nation, 42, 49, 91
National Liberation Front, 37
National Socialism, 5, 18
National Socialist, 5, 17
nationalist, 44
nation-state, 91
native, 40, 41, 42, 43, 45, 46, 47, 49,
    50, 51, 62, 64, 65, 68, 70, 78,
    84, 88, 89
Nazi, 5, 110
négritude, 50
New Testament, 45
    Mathew, 45
Noh theater, 31
nomos, 15, 103
normalization, 54, 86, 87
North Africa, 37, 38, 81, 84, 89

occupation, 54, 5, 109, 110
October 7, 109
Ophir, Adi, 109, 115
Oslo, 55

pacifist, 11
Palestinian, 37, 43, 44, 53, 54, 55, 56,
    57, 109, 110, 111, 114, 115
    Palestinian Authority, 55, 110
    Palestinians, 4, 54, 55, 57, 110
Paris, 51, 87, 113, 114, 115
peace, 7, 8, 9, 43, 44, 49, 54, 55, 56,
    102, 107, 108, 110
peasantry, 46, 49, 51, 52
Persian, 39
polemics, 6, 7, 12, 17, 43, 88, 95, 99
polemos, 7, 42, 43
polis, 3, 103, 105, 107
postcolonial, 4, 36, 37, 40, 6, 64, 68,
    69, 70, 71, 72, 75, 77, 78, 83,
    98, 99, 100, 111
postcolonialism, 4
proletariat, 45, 46, 65

race, 40, 43, 47
    critical race studies, 40
    racism, 47, 111
    racist, 47
Rashomon, 28
representation, 73
republic, 6
revolution, 6, 39, 45, 46
    revolutionary, 7, 9, 10, 51, 86, 91,
    99
Rosenzweig, Franz, 89, 90, 91, 93
rule of law, 8

Sartre, Jean-Paul, 37, 47, 51, 83
sati, 66, 67
Schmitt, Carl, 4, 5, 6, 7, 8, 9, 10, 11,
    12, 13, 14, 15, 16, 17, 18, 19,
    23, 28, 35, 37, 38, 39, 41, 42,
    44, 45, 50, 57, 5, 62, 66, 77, 78,
    79, 87, 101, 103, 104, 105, 106,
    111, 113, 115
    Nomos der Erde, 12
    Political Theology, 5
    The Concept of the Political, 5,
    113, 115
Semitic, 22
Sephardi, 89
settlers, 42, 47, 60
silence, 2, 18, 19, 20, 21, 27, 28, 29,
    30, 31, 33, 35, 54, 56, 64, 69,
    70, 71, 72, 75, 78, 98, 102
sin, 10, 15, 23, 39, 48, 87, 108
slaves, 43, 48
Socrates, 21
South Africa, 40, 56
sovereign, 8, 9, 15, 57, 66, 68, 70,
    71, 73, 74, 75, 77, 78, 80, 86,
    87, 99, 100, 103, 104, 105, 106,
    107, 108, 109, 110, 111
sovereignty, 6, 8, 9, 15, 57, 67, 87,
    100, 104, 105, 109, 111

Index | 121

speech act, 20, 55, 56, 69, 71, 102
Spivak, Gayatri Chakravorty, 4, 5, 6,
61, 62, 63, 64, 65, 66, 67, 68,
69, 70, 71, 72, 73, 74, 75, 77,
78, 79, 80, 81, 88, 93, 99, 108,
114, 115
Can the Subaltern Speak?, 6, 114,
115
state of exception, 8, 9
subaltern, 6, 65, 66, 67, 68, 69, 70,
72, 73, 74, 75, 78, 81, 88, 99,
100
Subaltern Studies Group, 70

Talmud, 103
technology, 12, 28
Tezuka, Tomio, 22
theology, 10, 15, 22, 23, 38, 44
Tower of Babel, 3, 10, 14, 24, 25, 73,
77, 95, 102, 109
translation, 19, 20, 37, 73, 88, 89, 90,
92, 93, 95

Ukraine, 11
UN, 54, 56
United States, 54, 90
untranslatable, 90, 93

Vietnam, 47
violence, 3, 11, 13, 19, 20, 25, 28,
35, 36, 37, 38, 41, 42, 44, 46,
47, 48, 49, 50, 54, 55, 56, 5, 6,
61, 62, 63, 64, 65, 66, 67, 68,
69, 71, 72, 77, 78, 83, 86, 88,
99, 101, 102, 103, 104, 105,
106, 107, 108, 109, 110, 111,
113, 115

war, 6, 7, 8, 10, 11, 12, 13, 14, 15,
17, 18, 28, 35, 37, 38, 57, 5, 77,
101, 102, 104, 105, 106, 108,
110, 111
war on war, 7, 59
West, 11, 18, 22, 27, 28, 31, 36, 69,
98, 109
Western, 11, 19, 22, 23, 24, 26, 30,
31, 32, 39, 69, 73, 74, 75, 78,
80, 81, 82, 89, 98, 99, 100, 108,
109, 111
West Bank, 109
Wink, 30, 31
WWII, 47, 108

Zephaniah, 24
Zionist, 55